The "C

Workb

*A companion study guide booklet
written and recommended to be used with:*
*"The Catholic Demonologist Handbook"*

© 2008-2013 Kenneth G. Deel

Edits & additions by Farah Rose Deel

Copyright ©2008-2013

## ABOUT THIS BOOK

The original intention of this book was for further study, comprehension and greater awareness as to the contents of the companion book: "The Catholic Demonologist Handbook".

It begins with a self-test of 103 questions, followed by an outline as to each question where a description of some choices are added, with comments, to better clarify and restate, why an answer may be more true than another one.

Please take your time, do your research, reread and ask questions. There are questions in here where 'one size doesn't fit all'. Also, the Author would appreciate any feedback you may care to mail back with this exam or even separately if you wish to remain anonymous as we are daily striving to do our very best and learn to the best of our ability.

## CONTENTS:

**About this book**

**Index**

**Preface**

**Section I:** The exam (103 questions, refer to separate booklet)

**Section II:** The answers with explanations

**Section III:** Supplemental material

# PREFACE / DISCLAIMER

The viewpoints, opinions, statements and all content expressed in this book do not necessarily reflect the opinions or current beliefs of the Author. Some names and identifying details have been changed to protect the privacy of the individuals represented herein. This book is not intended as a substitute for the medical advice of your physician. The reader should regularly consult a physician in matters relating to his/her health with respect to any symptoms that may require diagnosis or medical attention. The authors and publisher advise reader to take full responsibility for their own safety and know their limits. Before practicing any of the skills or methodologies as described in this book, be sure that you are confident and do not take risks beyond your level of experience, aptitude, training and comfort level. This work is subject to copyright laws. No part of this book may be used, copied or photographed or presented in any other public or private forum under penalty of law. If you have purchased this book to be used as "Exploitation" to be used against the Author, or any member of his family ensigns or heirs, you have violated the terms of purchase and will be subject to any and all legal action available. It should also be noted that with the exception of this preface and the above disclaimer, that this book was originally written in 2008 and any references of personal nature are do not remain in effect at today's current date.

## WHY THE RELIGON?

Some gentle readers may be put off by my direct inclination to orthodox solutions, not scientific ones alone. This book is geared for both minds, it is specifically to assist those who have tried science and logical explanation and these methods have failed them. Faith and religious precepts are for those afflicted by spirits of unknown nature. If this is not the case, then it is a matter for science/medicine or whatever humanistic methods you may wish to pursue. These books concentrate on "solving" ghost and demonic hauntings, and Spiritual warfare and in no way attempt to offer any other solutions that may be found elsewhere.

# SECTION I:

# EXAM QUESTIONS

### Outline of the Questions:
These are provided in a fairly simple context. Many of these, offering more than one option.

### In the multiple choice answers:
Sometimes it may not be clear if you are to choose only one, or several to cover "all that apply" this in itself is a 'test". Your memory is being tested to see if you remember/know more than one answer will apply.

### True and false:
These questions are as to be expected. Circle the "F" for 'False" or the "T" for True. Or enter it on the line.

### Fill in the blanks:
There are not essays, just a question to ask for proper words to be inserted into the blank space. Each blank space needs to be filled with the correct answer to get the question 'correct'.

# SELF TEST QUESTIONS

Please take your time in answering all questions to the best of your ability. Some of the questions do have more than one answer. This is a review, of what you've learned and what you understand from the workbook. Ample space is given between questions for you to make personal notes or jot possible theory or alternate scenario questions. Thank you!

1) **What is the main reason hallucinogens are dangerous to you? (choose one)**

   a) It's a moral sin to use drugs for recreational purposes.
   b) There are illegal to use, thus breaking God's law as well as "mans'" law.
   c) All altered states of consciousness leave you open for demonic attack.
   d) They can cause brain damage.
   e) None of the above.


2) **What old folklore does the "sleep paralysis" best fit? (choose one)**

   a) The werewolf.
   b) Alien Abductions
   c) Old hag attack
   d) Banshee
   e) Vampire


3) **Christian can not become possessed? True / False (circle correct answer)**

4) If you answered "true" which of the follow is also true based on that notion:

a) "Christians" never need to acknowledge the devil exists, as to focus only on God's love.
b) There is only room for one spirit to inhabit ones body.
c) When you are a Christian your body is the temple of the Holy Spirit, therefore nothing defile can enter it.
b) None of the above is true.
c) All of the above is true


5) If you answered "False" which of the following statements are true:

a) When the Devil shouts and roars at your doorstep, it is a sure sign he is not inside you.
b) Being a "victim soul" might entail demonic torture, which can involve possession.
c) Only God's express will are we protected from any form of Demonic attack.
d) None of the Above
e) All of the Above


6) What word describes in itself the 'What is deliverance"?

a) Banishing a "Ghost"
b) Uncovering a haunted history.
c) A rebuke of all evil spirits.
d) Blessing a home.
e) All of the above.

7) What are "shadow people"? (check which one apply)

   a) Un-manifested ghosts
   b) Demons
   c) Condemned human spirits
   d) Aliens
   e) Inter-dimensional beings


8) What number is MORE significant to a "demonic presence"?

   a) 666
   b) Seven
   c) Three
   d) Nine
   e) Six


9) Which is a skill that pertains to the job of an "Exorcists"?

   a) Discernment of a ghost versus a demonic.
   b) Determining if a demonic spirit is present at all.
   c) Investigating a reported "haunting".
   d) Determining if there is actually something "paranormal" present.
   e) None of the above.
   f) All of the above.

10) In a minor infestation, who might best be suited to help with "deliverance" if a priest is NOT available?

a) The strongest person you know.
b) The one designated as the "demonologist" on a ghost hunting team.
c) The home owners.
d) The most pious person you know.
e) None of the above.

11) What would a "demonologist" not typically do?

a) Field investigations.
b) Psychological profile of the clients
c) House history research.
d) Ritual blessing of a home.

12) Spiritual Warfare in essence is:

a) Not heeding to demonic temptations
b) The great conflict we often face through our lives.
c) Fighting urges to drink, when you are "on the wagon".
d) Dealing with urges of suicidal tendencies.
e) Directly combating a demonic presence.

13) Which of the following is more of a notable trait of a demonic presence?

a) Hoof print in the snow
b) Shadowy apparitions
c) Vivid, reoccurring Nightmares
d) Losing your key keys.
e) Levitations
f) Scratching sounds inside the walls.


14) Which of the above is more common to a demonic infestation?　　　　(Enter letter) _____


15) Why are (some) ordained clergy more effective? Which statement is more true?

a) An ordination intimidates the demonic
b) The self confidence that goes with having an ordination and years of seminary training.
c) The title gives the Minister or Exorcists more "faith"
d) The "vows" of an ordination is a special covenant with God…
e) Because they act with the authority of the Catholic Church.
f) This is fiction anyone can equally exorcise demons

16) **What is a Succubus?**

   a) Ancient Mythology
   b) A serpent demon
   c) A demon of Sex/Lust
   d) A Ancient Persian Goddess
   e) "Lilith


17) **Name all six stages of demonic activity as I cite in my book:**

   _____, _____,

   _____, _____,

   _____, _____


18) **Which animal is not as common for a demonic spirit to represent?**

   a) Goat
   b) Dog
   c) Cat
   d) Pig
   e) Crow/Raven
   f) Insect like creature
   g) Rodent
   h) Ape

19) Which of the above is the most common?
(Letter here) _____


20) What information can a demon attain from you if you are in a certain state of sin?

a) Your future
b) Your unrepented/unconfessed sins.
c) Your thoughts.
d) Your life history
e) The ultimate fate of your soul.
f) Your family's history.
g) You current mood.
h) Your physical health.


21) Why are some prayers are said "three" times?

a) The saying "3 times is a charm" is true.
b) In Honor of the Father, Son and Holy Spirit
c) Three times to better ensure success
d) Satanic seal are done in "threes", it is to counter act the satanic rituals affects.
e) Three times is symbolic of "3AM"

22) **What are some notable physical affects on "Blessed" water, versus its attributes "unblessed"?**

a) Smell is cleaner
b) Taste is more sweet and pure
c) The water doesn't grow stagnant.
d) The ice crystals form more artistically
e) It actually becomes even more "clear", according to light tests.
f) It shows a stronger "aura"
g) The affects on evil spirits and demons, dramatically increase.


23) **Why do Demons rare show their true form?**

a) They are shy around humans.
b) They are purposely elusive. It is true that they most often hide their presence to avoid detection, it is only by God's express will, that they may at times seem to get sloppy and reveal themselves. Or else they would always so cleverly and discreetly affect your family and life.
c) Their true appearance is shockingly, frightening. They would run a great many away if they showed their true appearance. It is said to be so frightening, you would naturally gravitate towards God, which in itself is highly counterproductive to their goals.
d) They DO NOT have a true and distinct appearance, since they are merely "spirits".
e) To show a true form is to be "Honest" and "True" which is not a character profile of demonic as to reveal its true self, and likeness.

24) Which of the following are only "Myth"

a) The use of Mirrors to expel demons
b) Faith in a rock is better than no faith.
c) Ghost can kill you
d) Curses do affect Christians.


25) Demons can't reproduce.    TRUE or FALSE


26) Demons are technically the souls of the Nephilim. TRUE or FALSE


27) Demons can extract thought and always know what you are thinking.    TRUE   or FALSE


28) What attributes do demons NOT share with many of the supposed ALIEN ENCOUNTER reported?

a) Memories of the encounters can be repressed.
b) Aversions to "Jesus" name spoken.
c) Sleep paralysis
d) Telepathic communication
e) 3AM/Night time visits more common

29) How many demons are there? (pick the number closet)

a) 1000's
b) Hundreds of thousands
c) Millions
d) Billions
e) Trillions
f) None of the Above

30) Demons are affected by household incandescent lighting at night, just as they can be "sunlight"?
TRUE or FALSE

31) Demons seem to "physically" enter certain regions and parts of the human body. (Check all that more commonly apply)

a) Eyes
b) Mouth
c) Ears
d) Solar Plexus
e) Anal cavity
f) Nose

**32)** Name the spiritual "Armor of God":

_____,
_____,
_____,
_____,
_____,
_____.

**33)** Classify the four basic types of a "haunting spirit".

_____,
_____,
_____,
_____.

**34)** Which are essentially the same as an Ouija board?

a) Franks Box, (Ghost box, telephone to the dead)
b) And "EVP" picked up on a stationary recorder.
c) A swinging pendulum.
d) KII Meter.
e) Obelisk
f) Table tipping.

35) Which location should not be so actively haunted by default?

a) A Bordello
b) A hospital
c) A grave yard
d) A funeral home
e) A prison

36) Which of the above is likely to be more haunted? (Enter letter here) _____

37) What alone is the main reason that you chose that answer in 38?

a) The sheer statistic as to the number of people.
b) The types of people who live there or frequent there.
c) The type of place it is.
d) "Death" and bodies

**38)** What is alone is true relating to what I call a 'back door" method?

   **a)** Systematically forcing an entity out through an open door while doing a "cleansing"
   **b)** Being so discreet in your intention when visiting the haunted location, even the spirits are not aware you are there to remove them.
   **c)** Saying prayers way from the active haunted location.
   **d)** Using Solomon's magic to force the spirit to leave.
   **e)** Having clergy not dress in street clothes, being "Incognito" as to who he is.
   **f)** Not directly confronting the spirit.


**39)** Metaphorically, which best describes why Cold spots more commonly occur at a known haunted location?

   a) A Carrier brand "Heat pump" removing the heat to 'cool' the room.
   b) Ice cubes dropped in a fresh batch of cool aid.
   c) And drafty breeze coming up from the open cellar
   d) A fan blowing to cool a CPU on a computer
   e) Winter chill coming from the north to cool the September heat.
   f) None of the Above.

40) What is mean by the term "Guns blazing" in the book?

a) Not taking your sweet time, during urgent investigation phases.
b) A severe demonic attack.
c) A "retaliation" or 'payback' from demonic spirits after an unsuccessful 'cleansing'
d) A early misuse of holy symbols, words, rituals
e) To always have allot of faith when you enter any supposed 'haunted location'


41) What are some more common night attacks one might find as they try to sleep?

a) Burning sensation from a phantom "touch"
b) Strangulation on the throat.
c) A suffocating weigh on their chest
d) Induced heart attack
e) A Life force energy "feeding"
f) Stabbing sensation on the body
g) A 'slap'
h) A poke in the eye

**42)** What are the five basic steps to deliverance?

_____

_____,

_____

_____,

_____

_____,

_____


**43)** How might a spirit enter your living space, check all that commonly apply:

a) Through the walls
b) Ceiling
c) Floor
d) Doorway
e) Window
f) Portal


**44)** A Curse will not affect a "Christian"
TRUE or FALSE


**45)** Curses are only the result of "Black Magic"
TRUE or FALSE

46) A Curse CAN NOT be broken unless you know the spell that has been cast.   TRUE  or  FALSE


47) Curses" are in essence" a "demonic attachment" TRUE  or FALSE


48) Pagans can not break a  curse with "Christian" solutions.  TRUE  or FALSE


49) If you don't "Believe" in the curse, it will not affect you!  TRUE or FALSE


50) OUIJA BOARDS – What of the following is True? Check all that apply:

   a) Ouija boards are not in themselves unholy, just a piece of word with a printed letters.
   b) If a spirit is misspelling words, it is a "demonic" spirit.
   c) Both Human and Inhuman spirits will communicate through the board.
   d) It CAN be used safely in helping determine a spirit IS present at a location.

51) **In the book, by "rebirth" I am referring to:**

a) To discover your past life self through transgression theory.
b) To become a "Born again Christian"
c) To experience an NDE
d) A Human Ghost that is aware that it is a Ghost
e) When a Human ghost is found possessing a living person.
f) To die temporarily, "Flat-lining", and to survive that ordeal.

52) **"Red eyes" are more often characteristic of:**

a) An animal spirit
b) Possessed victim
c) A demon of the "Black arts"
d) Condemned Human spirits
e) None of the above

53) **A human spirit can not possess a person… Circle all statements that are "true"**

a) Without the aid of a demonic spirit…
b) …Alone.
c) The can "inhabit", but not "possess"
d) They can not "control" the person
e) None of the above

**54) Lucifer is... (Circle all that are true)**

a) A fallen angel
b) The highest ranking devil
c) The one called "Satan" in the bible and by other references.
d) The dragon from the apocalypse.
e) The "Advocate"
f) The "Light bearer"
g) The "lord of the flies"
h) The prince of darkness

**55) A client tells of a "shadowy being" that is scaring the kids, but also witnessed by the parents. Based on this information alone what might you advise?**

a) Do not advise until you get more information.
b) Inform them, "They have a demon", and that you will be taking measures to help them.
c) Give them prayers to say, send Saint Benedict Medals for the family to wear.
d) Tell them to try smudging the place with a sage stick.
e) Tell them since they are Christian and believe in Jesus they have nothing to fear.
f) Tell them to ignore it and see if it goes away

**56)** A client tells them their child is "seeing ghosts", she makes mention that the child is a "sensitive". Based on this info alone, what would you reply with next?

a) It is via Hereditary "divine spirits"
b) God has bestowed gifts onto the child
c) A Family curse
d) The child is living in a demonic infestation
e) Child is chronically ill
f) The child is not (properly) blessed/baptized
g) Child has had a head injury.
h) None of the above could apply.
i) All of the above can apply.

**57)** In the book, what do I mean by "shaking the beehive"? (Check all that apply)

a) Taking action to rebuke evil spirits, therefore drawing a retaliation
b) Anytime you begin an "exorcism" or "cleansing
c) Provoking the spirits.
d) Confronting the spirits directly
e) Insulting the spirit as to get evidence.

**58) Complete this sentence; A home "blessing"...**

   a) Should never be done by properly ordained "Clergy"
   b) Can be done by the home owners
   c) Should be done with caution
   d) Is to rebuke evil spirits
   e) Should be done at night when the spirits are there.

**59) What is more common reason for a nine year old to "see ghosts"?**

   a) Via Hereditary "divine spirits"
   b) God has bestowed gifts onto the child
   c) A Family curse
   d) The child is living in a demonic infestation
   e) Child is chronically ill
   f) The child is not (properly) blessed/baptized
   g) Child has had a head injury..

**60)** What is likely the real reason lights may dim when a demonic spirit enters a lit room?
(check all that may apply)

   a) to frighten you
   b) They are feeding on the energy source that powers the lights
   c) The truly advert to light, and are dimming the lights for a certain 'comfort'
   d) There negative energy is countering the electrical source, thus canceling it out to some degree.


**61)** A client calls you to update you on recent 'activity', and makes mention that two days ago, at about 3:30AM, a black haired spirit appeared at her bedside, it appeared to be old woman with 'white eyes' it said : "Your God can't help you now", screamed as it turned into an appearance of a rotting corpse and it disappeared. You suspect, the story is not in the least all true. Why?

a) The spirit did NOT appear closer to 3AM, as an evil spirit would do normally.
b) White eyes are not so common and are rare
c) She waited two days before telling about something like this.
d) "Your God can't help you now", is a movie quote.
e) It is uncommon for apparitions to change appearance into something like a corpse. Even rarer for a spirit to reveal itself as such.

62) All human ghosts, in that phase of existence Catholics call "purgatory" would not be able to speak, if they appear to you. TRUE or FALSE

63) Poltergeist cases are more often "Pk energy" related to an adolescent. TRUE or FALSE

64) Demons can not hurt you if you are not afraid of them. TRUE or FALSE

65) Christians can be hurt by demons even with "faith" TRUE or FALSE

66) The Catholic Church teaches all suicides go to hell. TRUE or FALSE

67) A pact with Satan can not be broken…

a) If the person dies…
b) If they are uncooperative
c) It can not be broken, period!
d) Only by a Satanic rite to "undo" the pact.
e) Unless someone offers themselves in your place.

**68) What is a "Jinn" essentially?**

a) Beings of "fire"
b) A demon
c) A fable "Tales of the Arabian knights"
d) Muslim Folklore, mythology
e) A "Genie" that grants you three wishes

**69) What is the most common reason for a demon to soon return after a successful exorcism?**

a) The demon never left, it was simply 'lying low' for time.
b) The client became to falters from the prescribed prayers and daily practices.
c) A 'curse' is being repeated.
d) The deliverance was focused on the wrong person
e) They begin to resume a practice that was part of the reason they were affected by a demonic presence to begin with.
f) The true source of the "demonization" was not directly dealt with.
g) Only one demon had be expelled, overlooking 'other' demons.

70) The more common reason an Incubus encounter will often begin because of...

a) A person at the household current or past residence lured it in, through some form of sexual perversion.
b) A practice of the dark arts.
c) Fantasies of a "Casanova lover"
d) A type of "haunting" is already at the residence.
e) The person already engaged in some of what the church considers to be "sinful sexuality"
f) The victim does not take early measures to rebuke the spirit at its first signs.

71) Why should Holy anointing Oil or Holy Water be used over blessed salt?

a) Salt is not a "sacramental"
b) Salt is a pagan practice, like throwing rice at weddings.
c) It is better as a 'preventative' than for a 'cleansing'
d) Salt is not easy to attain, as holy water, it is not 'free'
e) Corrosive properties

72) Which of the following are NOT carried or worn for "protection" into a suspected demonic haunted location:

a) Saint Michael medal
b) Saint Benedict Medal
c) A Blessed Crucifix.
d) Rosary Beads
e) Sacred heart picture
f) Saint Christopher medal
g) Relic of Padre Pio

73) Which of the above are not specifically used for daily protection? (enter all letters)

74) During an "Exorcism" a demon identifies itself with the name of a known higher demon.

a) The name might be to frighten the exorcist into thinking he is dealing with a more powerful demonic.
b) The demon may be identifying itself by it's hierarchy, not it's actual name.
c) This is at least one of the demons name.
d) All of the above
e) None of the above

75) Finish this sentence, Objects...
(check all that apply)

a) Can become possessed
b) All have an "aura"
c) Can be "infested"
e) Can be Exorcised
f) Can be "cursed"
g) None of the above.


76) Based on the biblical passage in Acts 19:15., what can we validate this passage truly means?
a) Pagans can not expect to ward off evil spirits in Jesus name.
b) Only legitimately ordained clergy can exorcise demons in Jesus name.
c) Only Christian should expect to expel demons
d) Those of the Jewish faith can not use Jesus name to rebuke evil spirits.


77) Lillith is...

a) Is entirely a Myth
b) Was in fact Adams first wife.
c) Is the name of a succubus demon
d) Is a cat demon
e) Is in the bible

78) Religious provocation is NOT necessarily done to:

a) To attain information needed prior to the full Exorcism (Roman Ritual)
b) To force an evidence capture, EVP/Video/Photographic
c) To weaken the spirit prior to deliverance.
d) To force the spirit to reveal its presence.
e) None of the above


79) Which object or holy symbol will NOT alone have an affect on the Demonic if unblessed:

a) Pure sea salt
b) A "cross"
c) Pure water
d) A crucifix
e) A Saint Benedict Medal
f) Frankincense and Myrrh


80) What of the following was NOT divinely inspired?

a) Saint Benedict Medal
b) Saint Michael medal
c) Holy face" medal
d) The Rosary
e) Scapular

81) Which of the following is not recommended method of disposing of UNHOLY/evil items, such as an Ouija board.

a) Bury in a remote location
b) Conceal it in a bag, and put it out in the trash
c) Burn it.
d) Have it blessed, then store it away in a safe place
e) All of the above
f) None of the above


82) What is the best description of "Purgatory" that is most universally understood by those of ALL faiths?

a) A temporary hell
b) A Roman Catholic Myth designed to "sell" indulgences
c) A phase of existence between this world and heaven
d) A place of penance and restitution
e) A place of fire and brimstone to atone through suffering.


83) How many times are ghosts mentioned in the bible (if any)? _____


84) By its correct definition, what is a ghost?

a) Any "spirit"
b) A ghost is a demon, always a demon.

c) An echo from the past, (always something residual, nothing "intelligent)
   d) A human spirit
   e) Manifested energy

**85)　By definition what are the "Nephilim"?**

   a) Demonic beings made from human sperm
   b) The fallen angels
   c) A race of giant humans
   d) Demonic-human hybrids
   e) UFO aliens
   f) Inter-dimensional beings.

**86)　What is the ultimate goal of the demonic?**

   a) World domination
   b) Your physical death
   c) To influence humans to further empower evil.
   d) Your spiritual death
   e) To get even with God

87) If you had to choose one, which is the best to carry for protection?

a) Saint Michael Medal
b) Blessed Salt
c) Holy water
d) A bible
e) A rosary


88) What do we more commonly find with EVP and demonic spirits?

a) Demonic spirits like to ensure fear with "growls"
b) Spirits are shy, you have to beckon them to respond to grab captures
c) A sort of spirit 'prime directive' prevents spirits from leaving physical evidence, except under rare circumstances
d) Digital recorders don't work as well as Analog


89) Jack and Jim are debating, Jack says most cases are demonic, Jim says most are not. Who is right?

a) Jim
b) Jack
c) Neither one
d) Both are right, there are only "Opinions" in these matters, no right or wrong.

**90) *If* Jack is somehow right which of these statements apply:**

a) A demonic is 'calling the shots' behind most haunted cases, although it hasn't itself manifested at the haunted location as an "infestation" or later stage.
b) Any "haunting" would have to be demonic since it is clear in the bible that all will either pass onto "hell" or "heaven" upon death.
b) Jack in referring to the majority of cases that contact him for help, where he specializes in 'demonic' or more severe haunting cases.
c) Jack is heavily rooted in the fundamental beliefs, and is not speaking from case study or experience.


**91) *If* Jim is somehow right, what would apply to his statement?**

a) Most cases do not have a demonic sprit that has 'manifested'
b) Demon's do not exist outside of hell's domain; therefore they can't affect this world.
c) Jim has never run into a demonic case
d) Jim simply does not believe in the existence of evil spirits or demons.
e) Jim lacks a level of personal experiences or has not correctly learned from them.
f) Jim is a pseudo-science type who clings blindly to residual haunt theories, and notions there is not life after death. Only echoes of our former selves.

92) In the Study Book, where I make mention of "cause and effect" I am referring to?

a) Testing the spirits with provocation as to get an EVP
b) How demonic spirits will by default react to certain words, and objects.
c) How our actions will directly invite and empower a demonic spirit into our lives.
d) Of how cleansings/blessings of a 'haunted location' is affecting the level of activity.
e) How there is a lack of "cause and effect" under a scientific conditions when observing supposed haunted people or locations.

93) Which of the following does not apply to my statement of: "Our words are binding"?

a) Cursing at someone
b) Telling someone on your deathbed that you will watch over them for as long as they live.
c) Prayers
d) Promises made in the form of "Vows"
e) Lies, slander, "false witnesses"

94) What "demonic stages" did I add to the 'list infestation, oppression and possession"

a)_____

b)_____

c) _____

95) Which of the following will NOT open you up for a "Demonic retaliation", when assisting a client:

a) Talking to them on the phone
b) E-mail contact only
c) Solely offering prayers for them.
d) Sending sacramental and prayers by postal mail.
e) All of the above
f) None of the above

96) How many spirits can "possess a human at one time?

a) Only one at a time
b) If they are "Christian" only the Holy Spirit will dwell within.
c) up to "six"
d) A "Legion"
e) The number is unknown

97) What is a "Scout and roam"?

a) A ghost might travel with you, wherever you go
b) A demon has no limitations or boundaries in its travels.
c) When a demonic spirit has presented itself, but is not in the least infesting the home.
d) A demonic spirit that has not been given "invitation to show"
e) A spirit that affects more than one person, and at more than one location.


100) A "Religious Demonologist"…

a) Is a title created by the Catholic Church…
b) Was a title abolished in 1577 along with the office of the inquisitor.
c) Is a title created by Author Gerald Brittle to describe the unique work Ed Warren would do as "Laity"
d) Is a valid title for anyone who studies "demonology"
e) All of the above


101) A child is afraid to sleep at night, he says there are black "monsters that come out of his closet at night. Which one stands alone is the better advice?

a) Tell them to ignore them, and try to go back to sleep.
b) Tell the child those monsters are real, and teach him how to deal with them.

c) Do nothing tell him to not be afraid and to be a "big boy/girl" about it.
d) Tell him there are no such things as Ghosts and monsters. Again do nothing.
e) Tell him he is a Christian and there is nothing to fear.
f) Teach him prayers, etc. without saying what they are for.

## 102) Why do some warn that you shouldn't deal with "demonic" haunting case unless you have a calling?

a) As to be obedient to the Christian Church
b) You don't pick the work, it picks you.
c) IF you don't have a true "calling" from God to do this work, you will be 'affected' by these spirits in the worse way.

## 103) The Blessed Virgin Mary, is significant in "deliverance" and exorcisms because:

a) She is the Mother of Jesus.
b) More so because the history of the Catholic Church and their honor and veneration of Mary.
c) Her Purity is a mantle of grace and light against these powers of darkness.
d) Her hierarchy in heaven.
e) Because she is a female saint.
f) As Satan used a woman to bring the fall of man, God used a woman to help bring the fall of Satan.

**END OF EXAM**

# **SECTION II**

QUESTIONS WITH DECRIPTIVE ANSWERS

**NOTE:**
The "answers" on some topics will not be elaborated upon, as to not be so redundant. On others, I may add much more info to enlighten the topic further illustrate the point. Now, it's time to get underway.

**What is the most important reason hallucinogens are dangerous to you? (choose one)**

**a) It's a moral sin to use drugs for recreational purposes.**

*Any* sin(s) in words or actions we might commit will weaken our spirit from within, and begin to diminish our graces from God. This alone will make us more prone to attack, more "vulnerable" and an easy target. While a mortal sin is a more serious sin beyond what some consider to be a lesser sin such as telling a little "white lie"

**b) They are illegal to use, thus breaking God's law as well as "Man's'" law.**

This is another point and may be a sin that in turn will weaken the spirit. At some point we might ask ourselves how selfish is it to break the law and risk going to jail at the expense of the family, community, losing your financial security (Job, friends, church, etc.), or monetary penalties/fines that burden the family? We must remember that sin is often how it offends and negatively impacts 'others', not just in how it directly offends God. When we choose to sin against another we *are* sinning against God.

### c) All altered states of consciousness leaves you open for demonic attack.

As I said in my first book, when we impair our ability to stay connected and fully conscious, we are open for spiritual attack. Even to the point of being open to something as severe as Demonic possession. This is another reason why Spiritual Sacramentals (Crucifix, Scapular, medals, etc.), should be worn, to extend protection to the spirit day –and- night, when we sleep.

### d) They can cause brain damage.

The body is the temple of the Holy Spirit and it is considered a sin to be negligent or to be purposefully hurting yourself. Although this can be a good reason, the "main" reason is related to the spirit, not the physical body. Now we do realize some "brain damage" can be permanent and as the mind directly affects the spirit, this to can be considered. Some who experimented with "Acid" in the 60's, apparently had permanently damaged that part of the brain the drug normal subdues. So imagine you are slightly in this euphoric state 24/7?

### e) You might get high and trip over a real ghost.

The feeling of being 'high' and the loss of actual brain concentration and lack of verbal acuity will not only leave you open to oppression but may also cause you to make other very dangerous mistakes. If there are any 'haunts' around, the state of you being 'high' is a magnet for evil and negative energies, you will seen as a beacon and would not even be aware of any 'ghost' presence around.

*COMMENTS:*
Operating Room/E.R. doctors and nurses will tell of stories where the patients on minor anesthesia drugs became violent or suddenly changed their demeanor to a hateful, almost like a demonic possession. They have to be restrained, and when the anesthesia wore off, they had no memory of acting that way. It was almost like some other personality had taken over. An anesthesiologist will say the drug is designed to calm and relax. It is considered a normal although not common 'reaction' or an 'affect' of the drug by some in the medical field. To me this is just an assumption. Relatives have said of seeing a family member react. "That was not my sister" But when you understand how anything but natural sleep can put you at risk, this should all makes sense when you understand that. To disable your ability to can mean a demonic will hope in for a joy ride.

## Why is it temporary?

Because your current state of mind was somewhat defenseless, if we consider where a person would be psychologically. We must consider how a person will have reached such a state from demonic affects through stages of oppression to have a weakened the mind and spirit enough where the possession occurs. This drug induced state is often where the person is at psychologically, but of course on a lesser level. It is still a 'surrender', even if it is temporary. Physically, one subdued by drugs will suppress them physically, and see how they could be robbed, or worse and not able to defend themselves. Always pray for those going into the hospital; give them a Saint Benedict or St Michael medal for example. On a rare occasion the "side effects" didn't cease after the drug wore off. This is what you might see when you see in those old movies where the doctor talks of a patient as having a "fighting spirit". We do realize our spiritual and mental state can play a part in keeping us alive longer. We do chose often to pass on, as we learn through the testimonies of those who experience an NDE (Near Death experience). Sometimes we do make a choice as to when we are going to pass on. Sometimes it is egged on by a demonic spirit also. My advice is to not go willingly, fight to stay alive and in this world. When you go by God's will it's his choice, and you will go without control and make the transition.

We also find that some more chronic cases of Alcoholism, you will find people who tend to be abusive when they are drinking large amounts of spirits. This is much of the same as being "sedated", and this is perhaps why the drastic change in personality while under the influence. And this should be noted as well, that the demon has attached itself to the afflicted. It will more so dominate the psyche and the personality traits of the drinker or drug user will more reflect the mannerisms of the demonic/evil spirit. (This also explains "Blackouts" which alcoholics experience regularly.) Our bottom line we should avoid drugs that place us in "altered states of consciousness" and try to remain of a sound and healthy mind during our waking hours. Unless absolutely necessary (Medical reasons), and pray for your spirit not just the body getting the surgery. These things are indeed rare occurrences, but better to be on the safe side.

**What old folklore does the "sleep paralysis" best fit?**

**a)    The werewolf.**

The Werewolf, as it fits with reality is a "possession", or an outright metaphysical demonic manifestation as with 'UFO Aliens', that some would call it a 'crypto-species'. Some old lore has magicians having the ability to change into animal forms. One onlooker witnesses a woman changing into a black cat; this is assuming the woman was human to begin with and not a demon. But I would not rule out a possibility that one in league so tight with satan and his minions wouldn't acquire such extraordinary abilities attain by demonic favor, just as they can bi-locate (astral projection), what if they can choose to make their appearance to be of something else, less conspicuous?

Saints such as Padre Pio and Mary of Agreda, always appeared as themselves. Angels of God have in some instances likely appeared as a big dog to physically defend the individual whom he is assigned to protect and in some instances other humans. To witness the transformation is quite another manner, as whether it is of good or bad in origin. It is all in such a discreet manner, the defending angel as a big Dog, mysteriously disappeared after helping the victim.

### b) Alien Abductions

In this we are talking about one form a demonic might appear as, with all of the tell tale indications of a "demonic attack", which includes sleep paralysis. As I said before I suspect any UFO ALIEN encounter bed side that is accompanied by these trademarks which include "sleep paralysis", even absent of a strong sense of an evil presence, my tendency to diagnose will lean toward being "evil" and not "Alien" or extra terrestrial.

### c) Old hag attack

"Hag Ridden" is still used today without knowledge and understanding as to its origins. If someone looked tired after a long night sleep there were said to look "Hag ridden" or like a "hag". This is a reference to the appearance of an "OLD HAG" that would emerge from the darkness, the victim would be unable to call for help and find themselves paralyzed except for the eyes. It would sit upon the chest, and they would begin to suffocate. More often it doesn't take their life on a first encounter; it is a warning shot it doesn't consume you on one visit. But the morning after, the person is said to look "exhausted" or "lacking sleep" the next day, as it shows the affects of the attack. Succubus encounters have begun this way, a hideously old Woman with open sores about its body, a greenish complexion, white wiry hair. What some attribute to the flying witch. So it is clear again here rumor might have mixed the lore of a Witch and a succubus attack.

### d) Banshee

The Banshee, which means "female spirit whose cry heralds a death in the house" or "woman of the fairies", is based on ancient Celtic folklore and not consistent with cases of "sleep paralysis". Although many of the old lore has resurfaced into this modern age we'll describe it as a "woman", if it appears to be human with distinguishable features. (Read below).

### e) Vampire

A "vampire", like an UFO alien is just one interpretation of what is more often a demon attack or merely a normal medical case of "SP". The Vampire lure played heavily as

we see similar traits so we suspect these old ideas of the Vampire are actually from true accounts of demonic attack:
- *They recoil to religious symbols such as a crucifix.*
- *Often reported as lurking shadows*
- *Night attacks.*
- *They advert to lights, even lights being turned on in your room.*
- *The person feels "drained" the morning after the attack, and will find a need to sleep allot for a time afterwards.*

Comments:

As some sorcerers/practitioners of the occult can Astral project themselves to a given location, and draw the life force from a person. A bit of a 'Psychic vampire', you can see how they were too far off with the vampire lore, and how even the living might be in part responsible. But I feel this is very rare thing that might come from the 'living'. At the beginning of the earliest mention of this legend when the towns people began to report of a black shadowy being,
They assumed it was the spirit of one recently deceased. In one encounter the widow of the dearly departed had described the visitor in detail as her recently deceased husband. In short, the thought was to prevent the wandering spirit from leaving its resting place, by driving a stake through the body, out through the casket, into the earth.
Thus by doing so they would be destroying the dark energy by pinning them in place. This was clearly a

superstition, as an act of desperation, which has no ground in reality or theology as a practical measure for such an encounter.

## A True practicing Christian can not become possessed? True or False

Although a "True Christian" might be expected to live the life of a Saint, but we all struggle with sin on a daily basis, and will fall on occasion only to pick up our crosses and carry onward. Simply being a baptized Christian is in itself is NOT a safeguard from possession. Look how some supposed "Christians" justify Divorce, extramarital affairs, sex before marriage, Abortion, and greed?

On many levels, the demonic will find a way in. Just look how those sweet little church ladies can be known to gossip and slander their fellow parishioner to where the person being spoken of is 'black balled' in certain circles. These sins can be more abundant than we know. With the amount of damage that words can do to a person's reputation, there is good reason for it to be a "commandment" to not "Bear false witnesses against they neighbor". Some TV evangelists will have affairs with their secretaries; they will buy expensive car, beach houses, sport 14k gold rings all over their hands. It is clear "Greed" has set in, even if they themselves don't realize it, their congregation is getting a clear message out of this behavior.

Priests will commit acts of pedophilia for years and have it covered up and he thinks no one is the wiser, but God sees all and knows all and you can fool some of the people some of the time but you can't fool al of the people all of the time. Shouldn't a guy who has so memorized the bible, attended seminary, and confirmed certain vows before God know these basics? Yes. So this is a matter of what to be "Christian" really is. It is more than a title or a lifetime as an "anointed" one, who is suddenly immune from all demonic stages of attack and infestations. They have to live their lives just as a good if not more unblemished than we do. They are Christian as well. Let us hope some of these who preach this "Christians can not become possessed" are thinking the same thing. I believe that to say this statement is highly misleading, especially when it is said without the inserted "exceptions" to that rule, and the actual "definitions to what a "Christian" in their opinion really is.

**If you answered "true" which of the follow is also true based on that statement:**

**a) "Christians" never need to acknowledge the devil exists, as to focus only on God's love.**

We can never be so naive, to know the enemy is to recognize better his strategies, God's love doesn't by default protect us from evil in this world.

**b) There is only room for one spirit to inhabit ones body.**

One man in the bible was possessed by a "Legion" of demons, in other words "many" not just one. Our own spirit dwells within, and so when we choose Christ, so does the Holy Spirit also dwells within us.

**c) When you are a Christian your body is the temple of the Holy Spirit, therefore nothing can defile or enter into it.**

We have to remember that many believe that they are good Christians, yet they continue to live in mortal sin, therefore the Holy Spirit is all but extinguished in their hearts. There is some measure of the Holy Spirit within us until death.
This again is an idea based on a "perfect' state, which is one whom few in history have reached this level of piety.

**d) None of the above is true.**

*Only* God can judge what state our hearts, mind and souls are in at any time. We can look at someone we see attend church daily, and assume they must closer to God when in fact they may be very far away from understanding anything about God's basic nature. Church attendance may simply be from habit or for social recognition for someone. So if you hear of someone who seemed to be "Holy" and is afflicted by oppression or possession, stay open minded never judgmental in assuming even a pastor can not become possessed, we should always consider that which we don't understand has a purpose: "Except by God's express will".

The notoriety of "Emily Rose" resurrected the reality of demonic possession, by making world-wide news as it was brought before a court of law in which many witnesses were brought forth so that the truth of these matters could be brought out.

### e)  All of the above is true
Please read the prior explanations.


**If you answered "False" which of the following statements are true:**

### a)  When the Devil shouts and roars at your doorstep, it is a sure sign he is not inside you.

This is a quote from Padre Pio, it is saying that the devil leaves you alone when you are not on the right path with God. Think about that statement very carefully.

### b) Being a "victim soul" might entail demonic torture, which can involve possession.

Many saints offered their torments and sufferings up as a penance to God for the good of souls. St. John Vienney, was tormented nightly, in dreams and awake by demons. Although they make awaken the next morning physically sound, their pain and suffering was quite real, and we know that attacks that can be redirected to serve a purpose for God, but only if we do offer it up, and stay strong in the faith.

### c) Only by God's express will are we protected from any form of Demonic attack.

Although, we pray our spiritual warfare prayers daily, it is really God's will how we might be affected by anything in life we perceive as "negative" such as financial hardships, relationships breaking up, a loss of a job. We must continue to pray and hope for the best and be grateful daily while these darker times pass over. And at any time this MAY INCLUDE some form of a sort of infestation or manifestation of evil.

### d) None of the Above

This would be the answer if you selected TRUE, in the question of "Christians can not become possessed".

### e) All of the Above.

The above are a few reasons why question number four is false, so this answer would be the most true.

**What statement answers the question "What is deliverance"?**

**a)  Banishing a "Ghost"**

It is considered 'deliverance' if the "Ghost" or human spirit is a condemned soul now in the service as a Minion of the devil and his demons.

**b)  Uncovering a haunted history.**

Discovering evidence, or a previous unknown information related to a haunting may play a part but it will *not alone* mean deliverance. There have been cases where a secret area, panel or room something was uncovered at a location and the haunting seemed to no longer be evident. In other cases such a find would seem to stir up a haunting, or make it worse. Each of these situations need to be assessed in detail to determine the "why" of the occurrence. Discovering the problem is *Not* providing the solution, while "deliverance" is a "solution".

**c)  A rebuke of all evil spirits.**

This is more the definition, since we are talking about a need to remove *"EVIL spirits"*, whether they re human or inhuman, this is what deliverance is referring to.

### d) Blessing a home.

A blessing is spreading Gods positive grace, through prayers, rituals, the sprinkling of holy water and so forth. It is like energizing a battery; the room will be imbued with Gods grace. It is like bug spray for insects, roaches retreat, but may return when and if it dissipates. This alone can at times remove spirits that are negative by default, simple because they are repelled by all things positive, especially of God. A mere "blessing" isn't designed specifically to rebuke spirits. The prayers don't include a command to remove evil and unclean spirits for example. They are just designed to ask for God grace to "bless" the room or home.

Comments:
**How long will it last?** You can add to it, or help it to dissipate, all based on our actions, words, inaction, even our thoughts were might harbor. Each time we pray, we might help preserve this like a 'Hedge of protection'. Each time we bring our stress into the home, and begin to fuss with family members for example, the negative energy will counter the positive placed in the home by the Blessing.

Here again we are dealing with some basics of "positive" versus "negative" as I cite is a basic and universal way to explain how most of us work in a more simplistic level.

e)   **All of the above.**

Uncovering a haunted history for example, isn't a close to a correct answer, we have to remember to try to correctly define words as they are meant to be understand to mean. Deliverance is essentially to be liberated from evil spirits in any form. So this answer is indeed "False".

More Comments:
Deliverance is more a term used by religious denominations other than "Catholics" as Protestant "Exorcisms" began to merge throughout the 20$^{th}$ century, especially since tent revivals and Televangelism made the scene.


**What are "shadow people"? (check which ones apply)**

a)   **Un-manifested ghosts**

This is a bit a silly notion, if they were "Un-manifested you wouldn't see even a shadowy essence. I can define a true manifestation is well defined the entity is co-existing in our physical world, with one of the 5 senses, which is including methods of science that go beyond the senses. Part of this is they might changes their shape or form, for a basic cloudy shape to something more recognizable. This metamorphosis is just changing from one form to another. It had already 'manifested' when it made its first appearance in this physical world.

## b) Demons

Not always true that they are "Inhuman", however they will more often be human spirits, either way they are in the same league. A demonic will more often be seen as a "shape", disproportionate, long arms, 7 feet tall or more, robed, cloaked with a robe and hood, a tornado shape.
The "Tornado", Ed Warren describes a visit in Gerald Brittle's book "The Demonologist" as a "conical whirlwind" that paid him an unfriendly visit when he was up late working at the time of the Amityville case back in the late seventies. A case of ritual satanic abuse I dealt with in 1987, involved a boy. I won't describe the ritual, and I won't detail to much, they conjured up a demonic that matched this description. The boy called it a small *"tornado"*, and it *"picked him up by his feet"* and dangled him in mid-air.

## c) Condemned human spirits

Either or, these sprits will almost always be a human or inhuman spirit, but working on the same side as a minion of demons. The will more likely have human shapes and characteristics that are more easily identified, such as the "Hat". We have to also remember that it is called a "ghost" which is a spirit recognized as human but not recognized as one you know of from life from the past. These are ghosts in their raw essence the light of God extinguished, they are 'cold' also which explains the "cold spots' one might feel.

### d) Aliens

Atheist and UFOlogists can dream and live in their world of fantasy but the simple truth is you should not consider these dark visitors as some "extra-terrestrial being" or an "Inter-dimensional traveler"

### e) Inter-dimensional beings - Refer to # d

Comments: First define what a shadow is. You see it in the daytime it looks like a solid black something smoky figure, it maybe a more pronounced outline like a silhouette to where you can tell they have a hat or boots. Night time then it's time to compare the contrast between the darker room has the spirit standing out as "Blacker than the darkness of the room". They seem to cling to areas that are darker and they prefer it. When we talk about Shadow people in this book we are referring to this, not someone's perception of a spirit which may pass in front of a light. It is not merely a ghost without the lights on. It is a black spirit in contrast.

## Who must approve an 'official' authorized Roman Catholic Exorcism?

### a) Your parish priest.

Your parish priest might be with you the whole way, it depends on the priest and what the Bishop decides. But at the most, they may get things started, but are generally not involved at any level more than this. Just serving as your "spiritual" advisor and attempting to assist you on the diocesan level.

### b) The council in your local Catholic archdiocese

There really isn't going to be a council to decide what the Archbishop decides or whom he may confer with or get second opinions from. There would be a matter of personal preference not part of the typical "Catholic"red tape procedure.

### c) A Vatican Council in Rome

Rome will get a record of this, but it doesn't require so high of approval to get in touch with church authorities in Rome as to authorize the exorcism. There is also a notion the Exorcist will be dispatched from Rome herself; the Archdiocese will have the list of names for Exorcists that reside in their state. Which the last time I checked there is at least one per state officially trained.

### d) The Pope is the only authority who can authorize the "Rite"

As with response letter "b", such an extreme measure as to grant 'approval' is not necessary', and likely the Pope won't even hear about any case unless it is a high profile case and he hears it through a media outlet by chance.

Part of this is to understand the size and magnitude of the duties and authority of the Pope.

### e) The local Bishop

I have heard from many clients that their 'case' might go through the Catholic Church in the State you live in, but not further, sometimes I've heard that in some cases the local Bishop is undereducated as to what these cases are about and simply pass on the task of further investigation unsure of himself and unfamiliar with the process. Sadly, it is uncertain where your case may go, as many Bishops are for the most part untrained in Spiritual Warfare and Exorcism subjects just like most Catholic Priests are nowadays. Neither do some understand the pressing immediacy that some of these cases require in order to save the 'possessed' individual from further harm.

**When we refer to an "Exorcism" we generally are referring to:**

**a)   Any form of "deliverance" of evil spirits**

This is not how "we" will make this reference, although it might be the dictionary definition, which is really a bit to vague and universal for our taste. A "Deliverance" can be done to a person, place or thing, while an "Exorcism" is a Holy Roman Catholic "Latin Rite" prayed over and performed on a living person believed to be "possessed" by a demonic being in order to "bind" and expel that evil spirit.

**b) "Deliverance" which uses a ritualistic method.**

Ritualistic is anything done/performed apart from words, slapping a bible on their head, jumping up and down chanting, holding a cross to their face. This answer is too vague and doesn't specify Christian only, and it is more than merely the ritualistic part to make it an "exorcism" as I cite below…

**c)    The Catholic "Roman Ritual".**

This is from our perspective although the word "Exorcism" is used and performed by others differently; this is generally what we mean by it.

If any other method is used in a Christian practice, it is called a "deliverance" session, "Prayers of intercession" and so forth.

**d)    Any Catholic methods of deliverance**

Refer to #c, a priest/laity can use a variety of methods to attempt to rebuke he spirits, but as I cite in my handbook, we typically don't call it an "exorcism" unless it is the Roman ritual performed by an appointed exorcist. By the latest edit of this book, this may change if the current Pope Francis is sincere about his authorizing the trained laity to perform these 'sanctioned' exorcisms within each diocese. This would be a tremendous door opening to help many.

**e) Methods only performed by a legitimately ordained priest.**

A bit vague here as well, and of course an ordained priest doesn't mean they are an "exorcist" by default. And what faith or denomination is the priest?

**f) Methods performed only by a legitimately ordained Bishop.**

You don't have to be a 'Bishop' whom themselves may not be equipped with the knowledge, training or other qualifications to successfully and safely perform an Exorcism. Officially this is only left to a trained, ordained and appointed Priest.

**What number will you find is MORE significant to a "demonic presence"?**

**a) 666**

This is more of a number from biblical prophecy, or one Black Metal (music) fans, and satanic dabblers scribble as Graffiti on walls, sewage trenches, and school notebooks.

But it is more related to the apocalypse book in Revelation of the number of the beast. The number never turned up in that form in an infestation, oppression or any possession cases that I am aware of. Other numbers might have demonic numerology built in, with "666" we have "THREE (3) SIXES (6)" two demonic numbers really to make up one number.

**b)   Seven**

Seven is the sacred number of heaven, the only number we find the diabolical will mirror in a form of disrespect is 3, since it mocks the trinity. There are seven days in a week. The seven sorrows of Mary, the seven years of plentiful harvest followed by a 7 year famine as foretold by Joseph (Genesis 41:14-36). SEVEN symbolizes Spiritual Perfection. All of life revolves around this number. SEVEN is used over 700 times in the Bible. It is used 54 times in the Book of Revelation. There are SEVEN churches, SEVEN Spirits,
SEVEN stars, SEVEN seals, SEVEN trumpets, SEVEN vials, SEVEN personages, SEVEN dooms, and SEVEN new things.

**c)   Three**

Significant as a number alone mainly because it is in it's mockery of the Holy trinity. Satanists, those who directly worship and honor Satan will disrespect symbols, objects, all things of God and Jesus in their rituals. This notion comes directly from satan and his demons themselves. To

disrespect God is to serve Satan. The symbolic number thee with show often in a haunting (a place) and possession case (a person). A possessed might have three scratches show up as a result of its FIRST attack. It might follow with a number three after that three bite marks, 'three slaps' to the face. It seems most often this is an indication of transition. For example you are in your living room reading, three knocks are hear don your wall or door. No one is there, no one can be as you discover.
You might find that another incident where three knocks are heard on your bed head board.

**d) Nine**

Nine is significant to Christians, for one reason it is because it is the result of 3 times -three. There are nine mysteries of the Rosary, nine day novenas.

**e) Six**

Where seven might be considered 'Gods number', Six would be that of Lucifer and his minions. And so the occultist assigns '6' to represent the number of man, as the number '7' is said to represent the number of divine perfection.

**f) 69**

1969 some say is relevant as a date, the Anton Levy started the Church of Satan in '69. But the number "69" is more that reference to an ancient Hindu 'Kama Sutra' sexual position.

## g) Thirteen

Judas was said to be the thirteenth Apostle, the only one not personally chosen by Jesus. The Bible assigns '**13**' the meaning of "rebellion against constituted authority", plus the depravity that caused *satan* to rebel against *God*. The occult calendar is divided into four (4) segments of 13 weeks each. I won't get into more specifics, however we do find that this number "13" in the least does have some occult ties and superstitions associate with it.

I have heard enough tales to say the thirteenth floor superstition, has good reason behind it to be a practiced with buildings skipping over that number. It may be significant to a demonic haunting in general. But the more significant number is clear the number Three.

## h) All of the above

Seven and nine are excluded entirely; therefore this selection can not be correct. And again three is only significant apparently as to mock God.

**Which is a skill that is better suited to the job of an "Exorcists"?**

a) **Discernment of a purgatory spirit vs. a Condemned spirit or demonic.**

The exorcist is to expel the demons and their minions only. They will not be the ones to the do the 'leg work", they are more the "clean-up" person.

b) **Aggravating through icons determining if a demonic spirit is present.**

There is always a demon when the exorcist is called in, although a human spirit can also be present. We don't expect here again, to await the arrival of an Exorcist to determine the basic 'type of spirit'.

c) **Investigating a reported "haunting".**

Early stages of investigations especially are not handled by an Exorcist whom is the "closer" not the "investigator". He doesn't "diagnose", he "solves" the problem already diagnosed.

d) **Determining if there is actually something "paranormal" present.**

The hope and expectation is that all medical and fraudulent possibilities have been exhausted before the 'exorcist' is actually called in. He might note more paranormal occurrences during this final battle, as it might show it's full power in it's last ditch effort to 'not leave without a fight'.

**e)** **None of the above.**

This would apply since all of these tasks are not specific to the work of an "Exorcist"

**f)** **All of the above.** - Refer to selection 'e' for note related to this.


**In a minor infestation, who might best be suited to help with "deliverance" if a priest is NOT available?**

Comment:
This is theoretical, not something we run into likely in our lifetime. Laity Edward Warren, actually did this on many occasion as a last resort or in cases of emergency to stop demonic attack and to in the least ease their affect on the family and house hold. In many instances off site prayer will work just as well.

**a)** **The strongest person you know.**

Physical strength is not relevant in a battle against spiritual beings. However it may lend to your 'confidence' to keep you more 'positive' and less 'afraid.' Only as it might affect your self esteem and psychologically in a positive way, would it be at all relevant to this. But only is a small way.

### b) The one designated as the "demonologist" on a ghost hunting team.

Some team appointed to be the supposed "demonologist' is only an honorary title and such esteemed promotions will not better named them for the battle.

### c) The home owners.

What is bound on earth is so bound in heaven. Many things we vow or contact, are also bound in heaven. God recognizes our home we pay mortgages on as OUR HOME. And you have a certain authority no one else, outside certain ordained clergy, don't have. Each case much be assessed before hand to be sure a dangerous physical retaliation is not a result, or a financial hit.

### d) The most pious person you know.

I am not sure if I can even tell how to qualify one for a toe to toe fight with a demonic base on this qualification alone. But this is an attribute that is most important in an Exorcist, and is top of the list for as far as a profile of one who would likely be most effective to rebuking evil spirits. This person could often at best be offering prayers for the success of the deliverance.

### e) None of the above.

Not correct, as in "a" and "b" is incorrect. 'c' and 'd' can be correct together

## What would a "demonologist" not typically do?

### a) Field investigations.

This may apply as a demonologist is a specialist, but if he is able to do the investigation and one is warranted where as a team visits the haunted location or interviews the troubled person. They might be present.

### b) Psychological profile of the clients

This is a valued skill as a Demonologist is skilled in understanding how demons affect people he/she will also need to understand the psychology of the people involved and how they are affected directly by demonic influence.

### c) House history research.

Not a necessary skill, but it is never a surprise to have to do many things that might other wise be left to a true specialist whom is great at researching house and property history. This information might be relevant. These again are special skills. Not many can dig up the right information or might base their findings to much on hearsay or local legends and not enough on legitimate historical records. Most often we find house history to be irrelevant to solving the haunting. However, property and homes might be tainted by some past evil. That needs to be considered beyond the typical demonic haunting or possession. But here is a rare case. As I often say the "drama' just simply isn't there most often. Finding out a person actually was murdered on the property, a history of satanic practices or dabbling in the occult are obvious flags. True satanists are very discreet as to their places of worship it simply does get out as something an elderly neighbor would know. Just some dabblers might have lived in the home and the neighbors like to "gossip" might be all you can use from that source.

**d) Ritual blessing of a home.**

This is one reason a "demonologist" should be one who is more "pious" or "observant", because this alone can be enough to agitate the demons and drawback a "silent retaliation". This is where they can hit you where it hurts, you fiancés, this can include the usual car troubles, strange illnesses, appliance break downs, losing your job under usual circumstances and the list goes on. If you do this 'blessing', the demons will focus on you and find out "Who are you?". So it's best to be a person who lives the life closer to that of a monk in daily prayers and more than once a week at church if you are going to survive this. Going beyond mere advice and "blessing" a home is a giant step. My advice: do everything but this.

e) **Deliverance**

A form of Exorcism, directly confronting the demonic spirits is NOT for the demonologist, but for the "Exorcist"

**Spiritual Warfare in essence is:**

a) **Not heeding to demonic temptations like lust**

We will call this more "Self Control" and will power, although it is a part of spiritual warfare, it is not the more defining battle which has coin the phrase.

b) **The great conflict we often face through our lives.**

True, but we are looking more for a definition of "spiritual warfare' many, many things are a part of our daily lives. This is a very vague response such as if a child is asked to tell us something about 'Alaska', and all that can say is that it is in North America

c) **Fighting urges to drink, when you are "on the wagon".**

If you are an alcoholic, addicted to drugs, this is considered a level of 'obsession' a stepping stone to demonic 'possession', as one might approach a form of possession directly through self destructive bad habits that are usually already there. When you reject temptations to 'drink' as one who is considered an 'alcoholic' you are shifting the spiritual warfare to you side. True this is an example of spiritual warfare but not in essence it is the definition of spiritual warfare as this question is related to.

### d) Dealing with urges of suicidal tendencies.

No doubt a more severe level of spiritual warfare, a battle of self versus the demonic who will be egging you on to take you life and carry out your current mood or 'feelings'. I am hoping when people are more aware of how they are being manipulated in this sensitive time, by these otherwise 'unseen' evil doers, that the person will not take too much stock in the moment when these thoughts are strong. Ignore them, pray and wait for the moment to pass. And then, expect them to return.

### e) Directly combating a demonic presence.

Any battle with a spirit is spiritual warfare, although this is a more rare form, and there can not be a physical battle with a being whom is it's essence is a spirit. But attacks can come in the form of being physical and we might use intercession from God's angels and saints to fight back, but we really never have and power ourselves.

### f) All of the above. This can be a correct answer

Comments:

As with the cartoon representation of an 'angel' and a 'devil' both taking turns to try to sway you and each one speaking in the opposite ear, this is how temptation works. The more you appease the 'darker side', the more power their influence and 'voice' will be.

**Which of the following is more of a notable trait of a demonic presence?**

**a)   Hoof print in the snow**

I haven't heard of this since the Amityville case, and some of us aren't sure if this was something (deceased) Author Jay Anson was adding in to embellish the story to better dress it up. A result was some 'inconsistencies'. This is "hard evidence" and will be extremely rare. What might more happen is you find the print, leave your bag next to it, and then when you go back with your camera to take a picture. You find it has vanished.

**b)   Shadowy apparitions**

As I had said several times, this is not an indication of a "demonic" spirit necessarily, although it can be in some case. It might be a human spirit. But we can always bet they work on the same side, these spirits are NOT good no matter what sense of feeling they project. Don't be fooled remember, the devil can appear as an "angel of light" we expect a warm fuzzy feeling at times to come from an evil entity this part of it's trap. This is similar to those deep ocean fish with the lights hanging in front of a gaping open mouth to lure in unsuspecting prey. Beware!

### c)   Vivid, reoccurring Nightmares

We will have these at a demonic haunting on all levels, it is not a definite indication of a demonic. It may be nothing at all. Now if we know a given location or individual is infested with a demonic spirit, then we listen to other indication and these dreams might be more to note.

### d)   Losing your car keys.

I talked about before how they can affect you mind and you will be more distracted and "careless' enough to loose car keys, wallets, credit cards, and other things that apply to our average day or weekly tasks. In some occasion if it is indeed physical in the environment it will move these things and hide them, or they might completely disappear. The problem, here as with the dreams, this too can be something to note but we can not trust it as top in the list as a definitive "indication"

### e)   Levitations

If you have witnesses, this would be something. The witness alone can be trusted as long as their dreaming cycle doesn't involve more lucid dreaming that can be

confused with a true levitation *(dreaming while awake and so forth.)*
Try to dig deeper and question them directly about the way the sleep or have them keep a sleep journal for a week. Do they sleep walk? Talk in their sleep? Experience non-paranormal night terrors? Are they on any medication that may have side affects. Consider all of these and more, but try not to offend the person. Use your people skills so that you can ask these as general questions. This is standard to ask anyway regardless of reported 'levitations'.

**f) Scratching sounds inside the walls.**

Early stages of infestations will actually sound like an infestation of another kind. This is more commonly described as rodents inside the walls.

**Which of the above is more common to a demonic infestation? (Enter letter)**

**(b)- Shadowy apparitions -**

Although (f) can also be close to the most common, but not as common as the "shadow beings" that are discovered lurking about the house or haunted location.

# Why are (some) ordained clergy more effective? Which statement is more true?

### a) An ordination intimidates the demonic.

This will draw activity in some cases, but simply being there present at a haunted location or possessed doesn't guarantee this facet. When you have a priest or pastor that is so 'Christ-like" that their soul borders on the 'Mystic" or if they are as pious Saint Padre Pio was for example you can be almost 100% sure there will be a confrontation.

### b) The self confidence that goes with having an ordination and years of seminary training.

Self confidence or lack of it is a psychological/physical aspect that can directly affect your level of faith,. This applies to anyone, not just 'clergy'. We are looking for what is special about someone when they are "ordained" a Catholic priest for example. We are not to be confident in ourselves and our own abilities, but confident should come directly from our trust and faith in God.

### c) The "title" gives the Exorcists more "faith".

Refer to my point I make in how our 'self-esteem', confidence, over all psychological attitude towards life can play a part for anyone. A title given by man in itself gives no 'faith' in and of itself.

### d) The "vows" of an ordination is a special covenant with God...

This alone is the single *truest* reason for this. Making a commitment, and sticking with it, if you fall, get up, pick up your things and carry on. What made the kings of the Old Testament special before or after an anointing?

For Judeo Christians a special 'anointing' was a sign from a prophet who was personally told by God to announce to his people that this person was his chosen to do his work. This is why the term is used so widely among Christians and you will hear someone say they have the 'anointing' to do the work they are doing.

A covenant is a spoken bond or an agreement usually formal to do something specified. A vow / Covenant with God is a lifetime commitment that is rewarded with special gifts/grace to do Gods work. But these gifts can be lost as the greatest can still fall as is shown time and time again through history such as with Solomon through his many wives. So the priest must be practicing his faith and walking the talk he preaches as well.

### e) Because they act with authority of the Catholic Church.

Note the "Catholic church" is the people who attend and the members of the Orthodox Church community. The authority of the Catholic Church defines a Priest/Laity/Deacon whom with the 'body' of the church that is the essence of the 2000 year old church doctrine handed down from the time of Jesus walking the earth, as having received and agreed to this special covenant . This is why a Catholic clergyman might be more successful in the eyes of a Roman Catholic for example.

### f) This is fiction, anyone can equally exorcise demons.

As we read in Acts 19: 13-16, again this shows how one can not exorcise demons from the possessed, and not be a 'Christian'. This differs from merely saying Jesus name and an evil spirit reacts to it. The name alone affects them no matter who says it, even audio recordings in Christian music and church hymns will have a similar effect. But this is far from commanding in 'Jesus' name, that a spirit 'leave' the 'possessed'. This is still considered intercession.

Again, the level of piety and faith of the person doing this plays a very big part. So saying "anyone can equally exorcise" is not true because there are too many variables. Becoming properly and validly ordained Catholic clergy is just another one of those to add to the list that makes up an "Exorcist".

## What is a Succubus?

### a) Ancient Mythology

Mythology is defined as an 'Ideology in narrative' form. So in ancient mythology we may look for any angelic being or "god" that would relate to a 'sexual encounter' as described in some tall tale. This would also be in the same legion of demons as what we consider a 'succubus'. However, these succubus encounters are certainly not a "Myth" and not simply defined by 'narrative' tales told through the centuries.

### b) A serpent demon

Serpent demons are found all throughout history. There is the well known Medusa, with live serpents coming from her head turning every man who looks upon her to stone. Then the Melusine, a horrific mermaid with two fish tails or as some have shown a serpent tail. These and other myths are found all over the globe. While seeming very dangerous to encounter we have yet to have an actual verified sighting or evidence to that fact.

### c) A demon of Sex/Lust (sinful/forbidden sexuality)

If the name is actually relevant it would be a 'demon of lust' that portrays itself as a 'female'.

### d) An Ancient Persian Goddess

We might find some 'she demons' or 'goddess of fertility', or 'sex', in any of the "Non-Christian Judeo belief systems.

### e) "Lilith" of mythology

Lilith is a Hebrew name for a woman in ancient Jewish Mythology and found in the Babylonian Talmud, She is generally believed to be in part derived from a class of female demons. She is also found more recently spoken of in the Dead Sea scroll, 'Songs of the Sage'. She appears on a list of 'monsters' In ancient Jewish magical inscriptions on bowls, amulets from the 6$^{th}$ century CE and onwards, Lilith is clearly identified as a female demon and the first visual depictions appear in literature.

A Succubus is a demon who will appear as either sex to the afflicted, more so selection 'd' would apply here. In folklore traced back to medieval legend a succubus is a female demon that appears in the form of a woman more of then than not.

## Name all six stages of demonic activity as I cite in my book:

### 1 - Temptation
The stage of 'demonization' that occurs throughout evidence the other stages, but grows more severe as the person advances through each stage .

### 2 - Scout and Roam
Is a stage I proposed that occurs before an actual 'infestation'. Keep in mind that this 'stage' will occur at any time you are involved in this work and in itself does NOT mean that you are becoming possessed. IT does mean be on your guard, say your prayers of protection, have your house blessed etc.

## 3 - Infestation

When the demonic has manifested (physically) it is an infestation. Often a ghost haunt is mistaken for a demonic infestation, because of the human spirit is more or less working under the direction of a demonic spirit towards the demonic directive. There are no actual 'human spirits' working to allow evil. You will always uncover that a higher general in a demonic spirit is always somehow calling the shots. The condemned spirit (one who repeatedly turns away from God) in this afterlife existence has no choice but to be a servant of the demonic. And even do things they would otherwise not want to do, such as to torment those who were once family and friends in their life. I have said this before on many occasions, as it is important to understand your deceased uncle who might haunt your house might NOT be there to watch over you in some friendly manner as we see glorified in the media via movies and programs. Consider the not so obvious; it might be a minion of a devil, used to try to get at you!

## 4 - Oppression

This is when it (the demonic presence{s}) begins to physically affect the person, and zeros in on particularly one individual in a household, this is the oppression stage. All of the activity of an infestation will typically increase and become more severe after this point is passed. This is the most common stage people will wait to occur before they will consider calling or speaking to anyone about help.

## 5 - Possession
When it begins to control the person with (or without) their knowledge, this can be audible alone. Appearing to only come from their words uncontrollably and appear as if they have no control of what is coming out of their mind and mouth. Their voice will not sound like their own and may even have a very low growling guttural edge to the tone. This other voice might be completely different and only speak in foul languages, some that you do not understand. Be aware that any form of control they might do is a phase of 'possession'. Audible possession is more common now because of people unhealthy interest in EVP (Electronic voice phenomenon) and exposure to it as well.

## 6 - Demonic murder-death
We have to say here, this very rare and not the norm in most cases of possession but it is very real and a very real and dangerous consideration. When a person is targeted for death by a demonic spirit, very violent things occur that may appear as accidents until the demon reaches this end. This might occur after possession, they will try to kill the host body and or take others out as well. They aim for the death of the person and hope of the death of their 'spirit' as well, when the person is readily taken while not in a state of grace with God. This person may be dying with unrepented/unconfessed sins and is considered a grave matter and can be so severe as to be considered

death for the spirit whom may have allowed themselves to be condemned in the afterlife.

## Which animal is not as common for a demonic spirit to represent?

**a)　Goat**

This is by far the most commonly represented and any Satanist belief that the conjured spirit of 'Lucifer' himself, is often appearing with a "Goats head". A demonic spirit in general it is not common for this appearance to presented by a demonic spirit

**b)　Dog**

Perhaps the most common to experience is the sounds and imagery of a "dog". Begin spirits of animals are widely reported. A very big and aggressive dog is a fairly common 'visual form' used by demons.

**c)　Cat**

This is much more common as the form of shadowy silhouettes, recognized to appear more as black cats or feline in the nature of movement the 'shadow' possesses.

### d) Pig

This one can be a trademark to a demonic haunting as with a big aggressive dog. A person hearing disembodied "Pig squeals" might seem to indicate a history of satanic rituals may have be performed in the house or on its grounds or an individual living there, or one whom have lived there in the past. This is why it's always good to have someone do an abstraction on the property where the haunt is 'occurring'. Satanists tend to prefer a sacrifice of animals that cry in pain more, such as also with a dog or a cat to that nature they can torture for longer periods of time.

### e) Crow/Raven

Crows are sometimes considered to symbolize an omen. While most cultures consider both of these birds are representative of death and darkness. Depending on the culture queried, the birds can be considered good or bad. On the side St Francis was said to speak to ravens also bringing bread to St Benedict as well as Saint Paul, the hermit, received a daily loaf of bread from a raven as he lived his secluded life in a cave. We can also site history how a crow attacked the "Bad thief" nailed to a cross next to Christ after he mocked Jesus on the cross. So it isn't logical to assume a crow/Raven is somehow a more preferred symbol or shape for a demonic to mimic. Or that the bird is evil. When manifesting or appearing as an animal tend to most often be black in color, or dark brown. Always remember they prefer 'shadows'

### f) Insectoid

A demonic presence can bring with it some or any forms of an insect infestation. Sometimes the large instantly growing numbers of them in itself is an indication of something unusual. There may be other times it maybe a manifestation, rather than for the insects to all be 'hatched' to the given location by some supernatural force. While for the oppressed/possessed, it can also be merely a hallucination, that is there one second and gone another. Hence my earlier recommendations to seek out all sources and possibilities first before considering a 'true possession'

### g) Rodent

This is one of the more popular 'pests' to upset an otherwise 'tranquil' environment in any case study. As cited previously, countless cases detail the sounds of a small animals scratching inside the walls just before the final stage of oppression.

### h) Ape
This on is so rare, neither myself nor my wife can say we have ever heard of this in any case. An answer of ape would be consider correct also as with 'a'

**Which of the above is the most common?**

"**[c] Cat.**" Selecting this answer as well as the answer for:

"**[b] dog**" might be considered a correct answer, the question is more in not choosing the wrong answer, such as **'Ape'**.

## What information can a demon attain from you if you are not in a 'state of grace'?

### a)   Your future

Demons can not 'foretell your future' so to speak. They can seem to 'predict' by your current choices what your 'possible future' will look like if your continue to make the choices you are making today. Demons can at best only "Predict" it based on 'time based information' they know and are made aware of. Part of this 'psychic' knowledge can be an in-depth analysis of your daily habits, they can string together a good guess of future events based on your daily habits and those who interact with you on a daily basis. It's not that difficult to tell you you're going to fall in love when they watch you go to night clubs every week looking for 'love' in all the wrong places, you're bound to find something there.

### b)   Your confessed sins.

Through an exorcism session with an authorized Roman Catholic exorcist, the writings of the forefathers and the saints of the Christian faith; It has been stated on many occasions, that your confessed sins are unknown to the devil and his minions. Although they might still know your weaknesses, they don't know your history of these things as clear. Unconfessed sins is another thing, this is why we are cautioning you to walk in Christ and leave no blemish exposed to the devil and his minions for he will use every opportunity to use these against you. More on this topic in another book!

**c) Your thoughts.**

By default they can not access your undirected thoughts. Your mind is where the battle begins. Keep in mind those suffering from "possession" believed that the spirit could entirely read their mind. Remember these things:
 1) This might be a demonic trick, to further degrade you, but making you think that even your own thoughts are known by them.
 2) They will interject thoughts based on your past and current actions/choices/words etc through subliminal means and most can not tell their own thoughts from what the demonic has inserted into your mind. Even in temptation stages we face everyday. This is our daily task to be on guard from suggestions are NOT of our own mind or God's.
 3) When one is possessed a certain 'communion' that is taking place. Since the possessed has 'invited' them in somehow, the demons may be more aware of what might you might be thinking, However there are more indications to say even then they can't tell *all* that you are thinking It is more of making an "educated guess" from thousands of years of oppression of humans. They have practice and humans by natures ARE creatures of habit. It

can be safely said that for the most part the demonic(s) is limited in its access to the human mind in all stages of their influence.

### d) Your life history

They can see this and they can pretend to know you better than your own mother, they have seen what you do behind closed doors when no one else is watching, only God knows you better, but a demon is second to a vast knowledge of your personal history. We live in a fallen world, and the fallen have been given 'temporary' sway here. Keep in mind that none of us have any secrets when it comes to supernatural spirits.

### e) The ultimate fate of your soul.

Never. Only God knows the ultimate fate of a soul upon death. For this is the reason he gave his only begotten son, our free will of choice and at any time we may turn to him and turn away from our former self, Christ also swung open wide the doors of Ghenna/Sheol for souls to come back to him. For a demon it is another "Guess" based on information they know would other wise 'condemn' a man or women to their fate in the afterlife. If they are able to carry out a "hit" and create a circumstance to kill someone, or directly kill them such as by strangulation in their sleep. The truth it is still a "gamble" whether or not they may be allowed take the soul upon death. Only God can judge each soul. Many souls have passed on and are believed to have "gone to hell", when they have not. While supposed esteemed "church ladies", whom seemed so devout in their faith have condemned themselves somehow and revealed themselves to be a "Lost" soul, sometimes as they speak through the "possessed". Such stories are heard in a variety of ways throughout the rich history that is Christianity, Many of these recorded in the Church and assessable via the Vatican Library or via your own access to the internet.

**f) Your family's history.**

As with answer #d, it isn't hard to access any personal thing about you OR a family member. This is why I say never fall for a "Ghost box" session, or Ouija board when a spirit pretends to be a lost loved one. Don't go along with friends to a soothsayer / psychic / clairvoyant / clairaudient / psychometrist. Don't fall for the 'proof' by the person or divination tool giving you supposedly 'private information' you believe only you dearly departed would know. Demons are a 'collective' (meaning they *never* operate alone) and they know more about your deceased 'uncle' than you or he ever did or ever will, the will 'make' things up based on fact just to sway you to their side.

**g) Your current mood.**

The more you walk closer to God in your faith, *the less they can access*. However it is typical for them to know about you, *these things* they are blocked from seeing on the Saints. The Demons would see/feel a dominant bright glow from the Holy Spirit around the person and nothing more.

Where on us it is known they can see is in the band of 'Aura' colors around us. The human aura is confirmed by Kirlian (also known as eletrophotonic imaging) photography. At any time our current 'mood' is broadcast to them this way and helps them to know how to manipulate you better and assists them to see the fruits of their subliminal temptations when your mood changes.

For any demon it is a delight to know you 'caved' to their suggestions of temptations and are being affected with 'depression', obsession over pornography, lust for your wife's girlfriend, an insatiable desire to 'win' at the lottery damaging your family's finances.

### h) Your physical health.

As with "#g", the physical health can be, in part, read by your outer 'aura'. To roaming demons it will be vague, it will display some areas of health, but not the specifics. It gets more complicated than that when they can tell how black your lungs are from smoking, identify a deceased family member you are unaware at the time. This information is passed onto the 'psychic readers' who are generally paid large sums of money to give you a "reading" which will include your health. Not always is this information correct however, sometimes you might be poisoned with a supposed cure or given just enough 'truth' that ensures you will keep coming back for more. There is a good reason they call them mediums because they often act as an intermediary to the demon. Manipulating you where they would otherwise fail to do so with out another humans help. You will trust a human more so than a supposed spirits. That is the whole idea we are all susceptible to. Some people can be given have a certain charisma about them to convince you to trust them that is directly from the 'demon(s)' giving them direct information the 'psychic' thinks is coming from 'God'. This is part of their strategy, a gift of a Charisma, to further lure you into this trust.

**Why are some prayers said "three" times? (Circle all that are true)**

**a)   The old saying that "3 times is a charm" is true.**

This isn't a saying with Christian-Judeo origins. A series of three creates a progression. The Latin phrase "omne trium perfectum' (everything that comes in threes is perfect) conveys this same idea as the rule of thirds in writing photography, comedic timing etc. The most common source of this observed by Aristotle's poetics. However, as I said saying anything three times specifying that it is in the honor of the Holy Trinity is a good thing.

**b)   In Honor of the Holy trinity**

This is in part true, they are observed to honor the Trinity, yes, as I said. Always find ways to honor the Holy trinity, God the Father, God the son and God the Holy Spirit, the three 'persons' in one God. If you are not of the Catholic/Orthodox persuasion, just know that God has revealed himself through sacred scripture in these three ways. By honoring Jesus and the descent of the Holy Ghost upon the Apostles (at Pentecost) this alone should be enough to understand the reason for calling it the holy "Trinity" which means the "Holy Three".

### c) Three times to better ensure success

More prayers can better ensure the success of a deliverance/exorcism for example. Just as hard work can help ensure success in many things we do. However, this is not the main reason prayers or phrases are said in threes.

### d) Satanic seals are done in "threes", it is to counter act the Satanic rituals affects.

Satanism is a mockery and completely opposite in practice in many ways to the Christian faith, especially the Catholic/Orthodox. In the same way we try to honor the trinity they mock it or 'dishonor' it. In doing so they do blasphemous rituals in threes, satanic seals for curses are three yes, and what better way to help undo them with prayer than honor the Holy Trinity to counter the dishonor done through their ritual curse.

e)    Three times is symbolic of "3AM"

We have to ask, why is 3AM really significant? The number three itself, saying prayers three times is not related to 3AM. But it is again, a possible relation to the Holy Trinity

## What are some notable physical affects on "Blessed" water versus "unblessed"?

a)    The Smell is "cleaner".

This would be rare if it happened. We've heard of super 'smellers' but haven't encountered one this good! An Amazing instance: When poison made it self known by a foul smell and revealed itself in the contents of a cup of wine, the bishop rose from the table and blessed the drink. The drink lost its foul odor, and then had a sweet fresh smell of a vineyard. This could be for two reasons. One the poison might have been something more than a mere chemical poison; it might be a result from a curse. Sometimes poisoning occurred without the food or drink coming across the hands of a would-be assassin. I can attest that through some encounter with a local satanic brotherhood in another place where I no longer live. It is quite common for them to use a spell that causes spontaneous vomiting, and diarrhea while even sitting innocently across from the victim in the same restaurant. Some can do this without even passing near you plate of food or drink cup. By the same token, they've been known to spoil food or drink remotely without you being aware they are present, and it will affect you in a bad way by the time you get home.

Then later you hear of them brag about the 'spell', one you were unaware of. Although you may not have told anyone of your night in the bathroom afterwards, they were certain their affects have worked. Mostly because they have done it often before to simply get 'even' with someone.

**b)   Taste is more sweet and pure**

Refer to selection #a above.

**c)   The water doesn't grow stagnant.**

An 'Incorruptible', 'imperishable' liquid or organic matter is not impossible on this earthly plane unless by divine intervention. In other words it's just extremely rare, and we would expect a blessing only from maybe a living saint or an act of God to have such an affect.

**d)   The ice crystals form more artistically**

This is one of the most interesting things, next to the Kirlian camera experiments. To show actual physical ' positive affects from positive things such as prayer, a Godly blessing or playing inspirational music in close proximity of the water bowl.

### e) It actually becomes even more "clear", according to Ultra Violet light tests.

Might be interesting to note, if #d was true, we might see this affect. But to test it's changing of reflection, refraction and translucence for example, I supposed it hasn't been done or it yielded no results in a test. We would suggest Chlorine (Bleach) for this affect.

### f) It shows a stronger "aura"

From our Kirlian camera experiences, I touch on this in my first book a bit. It did show that prayers near the water or a 'blessing 'affect the aura that is visible through the camera. It is very accurate.

### g) The affects on evil spirits and demons, dramatically increase.

This is entirely true. We've seen in the "exorcist" how the demon was supposed to react violently to "tap water". The truth is in one example case, the possessed said "ooooh wet!" when tap water was dropped onto their hand, and react violently in pain when it was switched with holy water in a similar vial. You can't psych out a demon pouring unblessed tap water into a new and empty Holy water vial, and then expect them to react to a placebo affect. They would choose not to react to holy water but they do, and we can rely on this as a "cause and affect".

## Why do Demons rarely ever show their true form?

a) **They are shy around humans.**

(This answer is not worthy of addressing)

b) **They are purposely elusive.**

It is true that they most often hide their presence to avoid detection, it is only by God's express will, that they may at times seem to get sloppy and reveal themselves. Or else they would always so cleverly and discreetly affect your family and life.

c) **Their true appearance is shockingly, frightening.**

They would run off a great many people if they showed their true appearance. Their 'natural' form is said to be so frightening, you would instantly gravitate towards God. This alone would be highly counterproductive to their goals.

d) **They DO NOT have a true and distinct appearance, since they are merely "spirits".**

If in Luke, scripture tells us that God 'has numbered every hair on our head' wouldn't it be equally reasonable that God creating all, created these beings to be beautiful like Lucifer and the truth of their spiritual nature is so hideous we cannot even imagine what each one of them look like?

We believe that all of them have a true and distinct appearance. However when are we really seeing it, rather than to see only how they choose to project themselves to us.

e) **To show a true form is to be "Honest" and "True" which is not a character profile of demonic as to reveal its true self, and likeness.**

They don't lie, simply to lie. They lie for a reason to deceive, divide and conquer. The truth will be not a limitation or boundary; they are also tools of the devil as is job is to distract us to his cacophony of deceits on a daily basis. They will seek to manipulate anyway they see fit or utilize the most effective.

**Which of the following are only "Myths"**

    a)    **The use of Mirrors to expel demons**

This is a very popular occult belief, as many of these myths are mixed into the Christian-Judeo culture via the movie or TV screen as showcased in the movie "Constantine". Mirrors were more commonly used for 'scrying' or contacting and seeing demon. Mirrors have been used in many cultures in the belief that it can divine the past present and future. The visions that come were thought to have come from Gods, spirits, or the psychic mind depending on the culture. Neither of us can say with certainty we know of or heard of an actual case where this even remotely worked. We can't trap a ghost in a jar or anything man made in this world.

### b) Faith in a 'rock' is better than no faith.

Avoid some of the ranting of those certain TV celebrities and their non-sense. This is foolish, promoting superstition, and this statement comes from a "wishy-washy" man, to afraid to stand behind the truth as to not offend anyone's belief system. You can not please everyone all the time, without it being at the expense of the truth, it is a form "political correctness" run amuck!. Some of these "slide show convention jockeys" at the 'paranormal' conventions ought to tell it like it is to get the REAL truth out there. Don't become one of their ranks!

### c) Ghost(s) can kill you

A human ghost alone can affect your environment enough to cause a fatal accident. They would borrow their powers from a demonic to display more power. Even to affect a fatal strangulation. Easy to trip someone on a staircase, or frighten someone off a road to crash and cause the death of someone. Prayers for example, will really help to avoid their affects. Even when your prayers are offered for others afflicted by evil spirits, they will be better protected from physical harm. They are always acting on behalf of the hierarchy of demons, even it they seem to be acting alone. So I am not sure if a dark human spirit will ever haunt a place alone, there would always a puppet master over them in the least. Don't pay so much attention to purported "Psychic-Mediums" as they seem to eerily and accurately tell TV land all the types of spirits that inhabit a supposed haunted location. It isn't always so. A very good friend's ex husband spent thousands of dollars *a week* for a 'accurate psychic' to tell him that his wife was coming back to him and when she would. It didn't happen, but that didn't stop him from consulting others who took him to the cleaners monetarily as well. A demon can conceal itself from all 6 senses and *only* a true man/woman of God, by his express will could say for sure if they are indeed infesting a home or business.

### d) Curses do affect Christians.

This is another where people may sometimes define themselves as a 'bulletproof' Christians, simply because they were "Born again". Through the life of any Christian is never a one stop, one sided conversion or conversation, where you can live your life free of consequences once you are "anointed" with a baptism or 'gifts of the Spirit'. This is certainly a myth in itself very rampant among many 'born again' churches. In a series of consequences, your bad choices in life will not go unchecked. You will reap what you sow among your fellow man; "sins" won't just slip by unnoticed because 'no one saw you do it'. Every 'sin' committed separates us from God and moves us closer to demonic influence and their deadly affects. A "Curse" is just another affect from the evil ones, as they are the ones who carry out the deeds. Even if instructed by a human. Don't ever think you are 'safe' from such things simply because you were baptized and go to church on Sunday.

## Demons can't reproduce. (T/F)

God created all the beings seen and unseen. Neither Demons nor Angels can reproduce to create angels or a new spirit. Only God can create a new living soul. Therefore if the creation of a half-breed from some unholy union with a human woman, the 'body' resulting from birth could not have a human soul. The seed of 'life' must originate from a human father. The body is a "shell" where the demon, (who was the incubus), had sexual intercourse impregnating the human female. Sometimes the body is inhabited by several demons as it is not restricted as to what level and what number demonic spirits might dwell within. This is the reason many believe that the angels that fell in love with the 'daughters of men' came to earth in direct opposition to God's command otherwise.

## Demons are technically the souls of the Nephilim (T/F)

What some might refer to as "Demons" are not, even some online definitions of what a "demon" is not what Christian-Judeo faith represents as a demon being "fallen angel" having fallen away from God. In historic documents included the Dead Sea Scrolls, the Nephilim are described as 'Giants' that were born of the fallen angels having sexual congress with the daughters of men.

**Demons can extract thought and always know what you are thinking. (T/F)**

At some level, the possessed victim might feel they can read their every thought as we've mentioned before. This is likely not patently true, Again I would refer you to the elaborate explanation in answer in 22) c.

**What attributes do demons NOT share with many of the supposed ALIEN ENCOUNTER reported?**

    **a)    Memories of the encounters can be repressed.**

They can be, but more so if the mind was subdued such as in a sleep state, you thought you dreamed all of it, when it was real. Then there are those psychological defense mechanisms that kick in to protect your sanity. Imagine seeing and experiencing something so unbelievable? Some will faint, and the evil will be done to them as they lie unconscious. They awake later perhaps with no memory of even fainting, or they might remember up to that point and believed it was "all just a dream." Satanists are known to
use the "date rape drug" (a vets drug tranquilizer called Rohypnal) on their victims, which include children in some cases, as so they don't have a memory of being

abused in a "ritual". This is how some of the reported cases in which the women found themselves to be pregnant. All of the men in one coven had their turn at a woman who didn't remember this barbaric ritual, only awaking back in bed as though "hung over". The baby is later taken the same way for a ritual sacrifice again without the mother's knowledge.

### b) Aversions to "Jesus" name spoken.

A strange thing to affect a UFO alien don't you think? If you even hear of ANYONE describing a reoccurring visit or a form of an adduction involving in their descriptions a UFO alien or whatever. Tell them in the least to test it with they utterance of "Jesus" name. I had two cases at least whom I heard report back that these beings react like demons to that name spoken. Be leery of any bedside visitation pretending to be anything good or harmless. Test it!

### c) Sleep paralysis

Medical "SP" also called as a rare occurrence I find where one wakes up from a dream and the body has not yet connected to the brain as it comes from sleep. This delay in cognition by reconnecting the mind to the body can be quite alarming. But in reality, there has been no other things to report when it is truly a medical reason such as this. No footstep coming to the bed, dark figures, a sense of an evil presence, and so forth.

### d) Telepathic communication

Actually a two way communication, between you and the entity will equally occur with the demon as it does with reported UFO alien close encounters. Often they can't move, or speak and communicating in this way is all they are able to do, sometime they can barely move their eyes around to see what is going on possible in the other part so the room. Now you may wonder why we are saying this when earlier we told you that Demons can't read your mind. It's as easy as this, your mind and the thoughts you think are very powerful in influencing your mood or energy (aura). When you have thoughts of suicide of self depreciation it shows all around your energy 'print' that demons can read like a beacon and even unspoken no one wants to be around you. When you think you're invincible and on top of the world and in a state of gratitude and prayerful you shine and radiate happiness and that too unspoken everyone will want to be around you because of this happy energy 'print' We find also that saying a prayer in your mind or Jesus name will lift the sleep paralysis and cause your energy to brighten enough to scare off some demons. Some clients did some as to even put a picture of Jesus on the cross, or imagining themselves being embraced and wrapped up with the Light of God. In this we are not saying all accounts are always true, just that they can be and we are aware of many.

### e)     3AM/Night time visits more common

The demonic hour, is when a demonic spirit will have the most power, perhaps to better manifest as something it is not in a more convincing manner. It is the midpoint from midnight until daybreak. Ask yourself why would an 'alien' visitor need to wait until night time to beam in uninvited to your bedside to terrorize you?

**How many demons are there?** (pick the number closest)

### a)     Thousands (1000's)

If anyone is saying this is the true number, or they answer selection [b], tell them "I said they don't know their demonology".

### b)   Hundreds of thousands

See the comments on selection #a above...

### c)     Millions

Closer, but this still says you might not have read enough to come up with this limited number.

### d)     Billions

At the print of this second edition workbook, we are assured that the current world's population is over 7 billion. At least one 'personal' demon can be assigned to every person on the planet. Some have said there are over 6 million demons. This is not including their minion of human spirits condemned through the centuries since the dawn of man. In Fr Gabriel Amorths' book, "An Exorcist tells his Story", he is quoted as saying, "When I am asked how many demons there are I answer with the word that the demon spoke through the demonic: 'We are so many that, if we were visible we would darken the sun." – according to my wife – he's right.

e)   **Trillions**

An inflated number, Trillion would be 1000 x One billion, or "One thousand-Billion" Fallen Angels. The number might be considered higher since there are many who fill these roles with the demonic as "pawns" in human condemned souls. That has fallen since the beginning of man existence.

**Demons are affected by household incandescent lighting at night, just as they can be "sunlight"? (T/F)**

In *"scout and roam"* stages, when they haven't yet manifested to an infestation. This is truer. They are able to duck detection better so that you can more easily pass it off as 'imagination'. If you catch a dark spirit it might be because your guardian angel woke you up to let you see what is lurking in your room, so you can do something about it now rather than later. Lower rank demons can't suck up 'positive' elements so easy, they are the weaker ones, smaller, but will more often work in larger numbers. Some even noted sea salt that as not blessed might send one of the lower ranks away. When things escalate to a more severe level, infestation or onto an "oppression" stage, being discreet may no longer be part of their strategy. Plus, higher rank demons might have already arrived, when the lower rank demons are infesting a location for example, they more or less help to pave the way for the generals, the "devils" which might enter in later stages.

**Demons seem to "physically" enter certain regions and specific parts of the human body. (Check all that more commonly apply)**

**a)    The Eyes**

We have not come across an entrance through an eye in even research and study.

**b)    Mouth**

This is quite common entrance point. The human soul seems to depart this way from the dying body. Even OR doctors have reportedly seen the spirit exit in the resembling a small orb of light, sometimes the size of a half dollar coin.

**c)    Ears** – Not a common entry point

### d) Solar Plexus

Possession seem to more involve an intuitive or 'visceral 'feeling' from an entrance through the solar plexus, which is also a way that the human spirit has been reported to exit besides the open mouth.

### e) Anal cavity

Probably the least likely of entry points, we are talking about where a spirit might enter, not referring to some form of a sexual encounter, or incubus rape.

### f) Nose

Not a common entry point, we are also unaware if we can prove they might enter this way.

### g) Open Wound

When the flesh separates in more severe subcutaneous cuts, yes, this is a possible entry point.

<u>Comments:</u>
I mention how these spirits seem to be limited in how the enter and even exit a home. Through the door or window the way a hoodlum might enter is common. By the same token if the mouth is not open it won't enter there. And these spirits don't seem to enter through the body by just simply "stepping in", just as they don't seem

to often just enter your home through the wall to begin the infestation.

## Name the parts of the "Armor of God":

Ephesians 6:10 -17 This tells you how to put it on;

Girdle/Belt of Truth,
Breastplate of Righteousness,
Feet shod with the Gospel of Peace,
Shield of Faith,
Helmet of Salvation,
Sword of the Spirit.

## Classify the four basic types of a "haunting spirit".

### Good

Any spirit that either has a chance at heaven or has been allowed to come from back Heaven somehow. This more refers to "human spirits". Since the Angels of God and the Saints aren't known to linger and actually "Haunt" a house for example. Catholics refer to these as "Purgatory spirits" to understand why Ghosts might be here. We personally recommend reading *"The Poor souls" by Maria Simma,* to get a closer look at "ghosts" of this type.

## Evil

Evil will be any other spirit who doesn't apply to the above. All are minions of the devil and his demons. And regardless if or not they 'appear' or even feel "evil". They are classified by the company they keep and by their very nature. There are no grey areas in the after life either you are for God or against his divine order. You are either on your way to heaven or condemned to serve and be the slave of demonic beings in their hellish world. More often as a "condemned soul, you are out doing their dirty work.

## Human

Self explanatory, if the sprit was once human, born and died, they are in the category: "Human".

## Inhuman

We are only concerned with the affects of the evil ones known as Demons and Devils, they all work for the same side. So for understanding our point of this reality when we say "Inhuman" we are referring to "Demons" and a very specific Type: Evil

Comment:
This is all we need to know to solve <u>ANY</u> haunting case. To quote something I previously said in another article. *"We seek deliverance from evil spirits, and seek to help deliver supposed good spirits"*

**Which of these do essentially the same thing as an Ouija board?**

a)  **Franks Box, (Ghost radio box)**

Comments: Imagine what device may come that a demonic/evil entity will be able to 'puppeteer', or 'manipulate' just to get at you. Transformers had a 'Bumblebee" switch between radio stations to piece together intelligible phrases of communication as his "voice" was damaged. If I hear a dead uncle suddenly come through the local broadcast of *"98 FM"*, I am not going to get curious and act like an FM radio is the latest Ouija board and go gallivanting around haunted locations as though it is a serious piece of scientific equipment. Anymore than I would a doll once affected by a demonic to move and dance is to be exploited for entertainment purposes. The point is the demon can make anything talk, it doesn't mean it is to be respected or made credible as if it were a scientific reality we could get the same results from qualifying it for regular use in investigation work.

b)  **An "EVP" picked up on a stationary recorder.**

Therein lies a controversy for would-be "Ghost hunters". Is this practice necromancy? First, why are you there to begin with? Serving God doing charitable works? If you can answer "Yes" to the above, simply lay the recorder in a fixed position, leave it and return later, and soon discover a ghostly, "Unexplained" voice or sound on the tape. This is NOT necromancy. Just as with any of these "ghost hunts" or similar endeavors to find evidence or help validate a haunting, it can get risky when you begin to look for these 'captures' for the wrong reasons. Also we must consider our motives as morbidly being mere curiosity, or an unhealthy interest.

**c)   A swinging pendulum.**

Pendulums have been used for centuries. Here's a brief history. The first scientific written use is found in the first century of a seismometer device in the Han dynasty by Zhang Heng, and then later made popular in 1602 by Galileo Galilei and by 1652 used primarily for pendulum clocks. Then later in 1851 Jean Bernard Leon Foucault demonstrated the plane of oscillation of a pendulum like a gyroscope, tends to stay constant regardless of the motion of the pivot and that it could be used to demonstrate the rotation of the earth. This discovery was so popular the 'large' version of the Foucault pendulum attracted people to cities where they were on display. This is the science behind the pendulum.

For our intents and purposes here, we are referring to the pendulum as it has been used for 'dowsing'. Dowsing is a 'type' of divination used in an attempt to locate water, buried treasure, oil, gravesites and tell your 'subconscious; desires. This sort of 'divination' became popular in the 15th century. By 1538 Luther claimed it was 'Satanic'.

In 1622 dowsing (with rods and pendulums) was declared to be superstitious and satanic by a Jesuit, Gaspar Schott. He later stated publicly that he wasn't really sure that the devil was always responsible for the movement of the 'rod'. In the south of France in the 17$^{th}$ century locals used it for tracking criminals and heretics of the Church. Its blatant abuse led to a decree of the Inquisition in 1701 forbidding its use for purposes of justice.

Now in modern usage by psychics and others, pendulums are used to determine "Boy" or "Girl" babies held over the expectant mothers tummy. The old 1970's had "Kreskin's ESP game" and it would have the pendulum swing to select letters and number on a circle diagram while the pendulum starts in a still position in the center. This is again a "sensitivity" device, and yes, essentially the same as an Ouija board. Not to be used for any reason.

**d)   K II Meter.**

Under the guise of a 'scientific device', this is another *flash* once for "yes", twice for "no" gizmo, and is quite simplistic in its design. For the common haunt "investigator", if it is not an EMF meter it is a KII. No doubt inspired by analog EMF meters that might respond with a swing of the needle, once for "Yes" twice for "No". This KII is used for spirit communication, where the EMF meter is commonly not, nor is it designed to be used in that matter. As I mentioned previously, the Ouija is direct from the factory a 'profane object' because it is specifically designed for spirit communication. The KII and some of these other devices will also apply to some extent and can be used to contact spirits as well. The EVP meter is design to pick up 60HZ EMFs, and I am still not sure why they use something so limited to try to detect anomalies in stray electromagnetic energy. In radio it is referred to as a "broad-band receiver", a signal strength meter, only needs a broadband amp at an input and an antenna of a sort, and we can fire it off with CB, intercoms, walk talkies, RC race cars, etc. The KII not only opens the door for fraudulent ghost experiences, it is also far to sensitive for even the scientific community to take seriously. So with "franks box" we get something so precise it can scan for and assemble speech from random radio broadcasts. So why is there a need for the KII to be so much of a "broadband" receiver?

e) **Obelesque**

This is basically an old fashioned Voice box synthesizer, This one will allow the spirit to manipulate it as to select from a sound bank of voice synthesized words, I think there is said to be over 300 words in the memory rom. A Robot sound synth voice ads to the drama. An internal algorithm fires off the box as to select a stored word randomly. These are partially influenced on changes in EMF fields. There are actually Android and Apple aps for your smart phone that do similar things.

## f) Table tipping.

Really? A favorite séance' method, there are a variety of ways to get answers. One time for yes, twice for no response can be attained in a variety of ways, knocks on the wall and so forth. This is easily manipulated by the 'medium' and the 'plant' across from them. It is all still "necromancy", and "Spirit communication."

Comments: Commercial stickers came out that you could affix to the inside of your cell phone battery lid that were suppose to boost cell phone signals. Another goes on the speaker of the cell phone to "divert potentially harmful radiation", these things were ALL cons, even the federal government found these to be fraudulent. For the devil(s), these are simple lures, no matter if they work or not, they still tempt one to an unhealthy fascination.

**Which location would not be so actively haunted by default.**

### a) A Bordello

The cries of the lost souls reside in places where human flesh trafficking is exploited. The Judeo Christian faith would consider it a prime place of "sinful sexuality", a good reason people might draw demonic influence and its affects. Purgatory spirits might choose to linger here if this is the act that holds them back from passing onto heaven.

### b) A hospital

You might equate "Death" "Pain & Suffering" to a hospital and its halls and say this is enough to make it haunted. Consider the 'death' isn't by a murderous hand. People realize when in a hospital that they may not "make it" through tragedy, nor is it unexpected. People often face their own mortality simply by visiting a loved one.

### c) A grave yard

With unholy acts that can be committed in a graveyard in the form of ritual occult practices. It is widely told how some lingering spirits will visit their own gravesite. This alone doesn't mean the graveyard is haunted nor is a chosen place a spirit may roam. That isn't what defines a "haunting". The person might have been what we consider "evil" in life, in these days, souls of the damned might just cling to where their bodies are. After all the body itself, was the shell that house the condemned spirit. With its own hands, it committed grave acts of sin which could have included murder. No doubt the more evil the person, the more tainted with an "evil" footprint. Just as an object can become "profane" simply because it was used for evil. Their body though empty and corrupt is to a profane object. As in a desecration of a grave site, might include vandalizing, robbing the grave, disrespecting in some manner, we can't assume every grave has been desecrated in such a matter. As I point out in the "Handbook" this can be cause for one to become "Haunted", more likely directed to the person who did the act. Especially if they take something from the site, a spirit attachment might come with that object, but the grave site itself may not become suddenly a site of an "apparition" by default. Unless the circumstance arises as to a body being separated from its parts, or one of its parts are stolen for some sort of macabre souvenir by the robber. These are more extreme and rare and uncommon, the same as with the notion of the grave being once a site of a Devil worship ritual. In short, graveyards by default are not typically going to be haunted simply because it is a "Graveyard". So this is not the correct answer to the question.

### d) A funeral home

As we mentioned about with a "graveyard", there is no reason for this one to apply, unless the person is practicing the dark arts, body theft and resale, or into some vile practice such as necrophilia. If you look deeper you will find another reason. The spilling of the blood of evil people who might have passed through there will affect the room to some extend.

### e) A prison estate.

This and the nature of the many who are residents of this colony are evident in just the name: prison denoting the sate of the human condition for breaking the law of the common good. It is as simple as what they have done to be put in prison and what they really do when they are there. Suicides, murder, sinful sexuality, the emotions of hate, fear, resentment, loneliness, there are many negative emotions that may still dwell within the walls of a prison. Every one of these is a direct lure for evil spirits to come and party. The very nature of many who are in prison for a time, they are there against their will. Many mental breakdowns occur from 'solitary confinement' places in prisons. The issue of medical or spiritual help for those imprisoned is sometimes never addressed. You can expect the re to be a direct correlation to the age of the prison and the severity of crimes and mental oppressions of the previously housed inmates. This will give it a stronger likelihood of being haunted.

Most likely the usual "shadows" not typically the grey ghost in human forms. Just the "silhouettes" is more often what is reported. Because of the years and years of 'Negative" with no "Positive" inside a prison, it is usually tainted with a very palpable certain evil, that only lends itself to make this more of a faraday cage of dark spirits. In such a place, no one is expected to be happy, hopeful, loving, caring, sensitive or praying, or much less looking forward to tomorrow… A sad, sad place…

### f)   An old abandoned Christian church

Old empty Christian Churches, more so ones of the older abandoned Catholic and Orthodox faith, are often discreetly used for Satanic practices. Some of the older churches in Europe for example, were built over unholy ground, as to offset the "evil" that was buried below This is saying that this is beyond only being a " Type Good

Human"; would haunt this place. That would depend strongly on the fate of the soul(s) that frequented the location. Remember a spirit has a stronger domain and a good "foot hold" in a building where it once dwelled in life. But this is true of any residence, not necessarily a church more. So this would not be the most correct choice

**Which of the above list is likely to be the most haunted? (Enter letter here)**

**[e]  A Prison**
For some it may be clear because of the type of people who are held captive there with little hope of redemption. There is a certain higher level of negative energy left over from these sad souls of stress, depression, anger, hate, sinful sexuality, etc.

**What alone is the reason that you chose the answer in 38?**

**a)  The sheer statistic as to the number of people.**

Perhaps an odds on favorite in this, since we understand that more sad inhabitants, the more likely, but this is not the answer that is the most true.

**b) The types of people who live there or frequent there.**

The assumed dark nature of the inhabitants surely will play a part.

**c) The type of place it is.**

Not so much the type as it is the mental and spiritual state of the people that frequent the area

**d) "Death" and bodies.**

Every mortuary and hospital would be extensively haunted if this was true.

**e) All of the above**

How many can play a part but 'type' of people is as important as the 'quantity' of people, certainly the 'type' of place. Just as importantly "death and "bodies" you might say at first but most prisons had a death penalty at some point, and many have died in prison. Only one room in a hospital might have a history of a patient committing suicide, but you really might have a hard time getting a story of a supposed ghost sighting from that room. And such a deed in itself doesn't warrant a haunting, even though it can open the door for one, tainting the room.

## What method below is true in relation to what I call a "back door" method?

### a) Systematically forcing an entity out through an open door while doing a "cleansing"

As I have said these spirits seem to be restricted by certain boundaries which include the way some must 'initially' enter or exit by some form of 'invitation', through a door way or window. Some report this is symbolic as the tell tale "knocks" you might hear just before an "Infestation" begins. However, this is not what I call a "backdoor" method. I am referring more refer to the phrase "painted into a corner", where you 'spiritually' force the entity to one location and out through a door just as any critter whom might reckless run about the house. A systematic method to flush them out and divert them to an open exit is a good alternate plan. However, I don't refer to this as a "back door" method.

### b) Being so discreet in your intention when visiting the haunted location, even the spirits are not aware you are there to remove them.

We can't really sneak past them, or wear a cleaver disguise they can't see through. It is only by special grace it is said the identity of Jesus as the son of God was masked to where even demons did not know who he was. There were indications he was 'special' but the demons were not in the know of who he really was, and likely of any part of his mission until he began his ministry at 30 yrs of age.

### c) Saying prayers away from the active haunted location.

This is good advice when dealing with a location that has a potential infestation or worse. Until we can accurately assess what level it has reached. It is better stay safe than sorry and take some extra measures in prayers for example, away from the premises that will not provoke retaliation. If not, retaliation occurs by morning it will likely not occur and you have successfully "tested the waters". People have continued to pray away from the home and over a period of a couple of months the activity began to diminish on that intersession to Heaven alone. So there isn't always a need to confront these things directly on their turf. It is called *"Back door"* based on the way hackers used to find ways to hack into older computers, it is taking action discreetly without stirring them up or aggravating them to defensive action.

### d) Using Solomon's magic to force the spirit to leave

People in church today forget the significance of Solomon in the bible as he is an example of how one who was gifted and favored by God, and due to the many temptations of his wives in search for peace fell so far from grace. Solomon's supposed 'magic' is a legend and that's all!. There is no evidence in any Talmudic, Midrashim, kabbalah or Dead Sea scroll writing that supports his relationship to magic or daemons. Don't bother reading "The lesser keys of Solomon" and expect it to be anything but 'conjured' imaginings to demonology. It wasn't concocted until the 15$^{th}$ century with direct evidence to this being the so called 'names of the demons' being given French royalty titles. King Solomon was born 900 years before Christ and the prayers written within to Christ would not have been in existence either. Studying 'demonic conjuring' books and other magical tomes will NOT help us in fending off evil. We can not learn from their side, they will only teach you what they want you to believe in order to manipulate you.

First define what the 'shadow' actually is. You see it in the daytime it looks like a solid black something smoky figure, it maybe a more pronounced outline like a silhouette to where you can tell they have a hat or boots. At night time compare it in the contrast between the darker room that has the spirit standing out as "Blacker than the darkness of the room". When we talk about 'Shadow people' in this book we are referring to this, not someone's perception of a spirit which may pass in front of a light. It is not merely a ghost without the lights on. It is a black evil spirit.

No information will come from the side of the demonic that can be used against them. Everything about them is deception and about steering you away from the truth. Solomon had many wives who worshipped other Gods, he loved them and tolerated the practice of their rites in his temple. He went from tolerating to practicing it with his wives. Prolonged exposure to anything impure and not good for your spiritually will eventually wear your resistance to it down. Never expect to expose yourself to something and not have a little of it rub off onto you in a negative way. The proclamation spoken aloud that "I am a Christian" isn't enough, don't allow yourself to be tempted. Avoid any "occasion" of sin to steer clear of falling from grace and being without God's divine Spirit. Solomon is all his gifts of wisdom didn't see it coming, and a result he is now a poster boy for one who has fallen to the "dark side" right next with Anakin Skywalker. A very classic and tragic story to be told, expect Solomon was very real.

**e) Having clergy not dressed in street clothes, being "Incognito" as to who he is.**

As with #b, we can't hide our true identities from these spirits, just because we might dress differently. A misconception can possibly come from the way a priest might be wearing a cross/Crucifix or bring items that are provoking the spirits as soon as he enters the building. Laying down your cross at the door step to not stir the entities is a better way to look at that. But a disguise would mean nothing unless it will entail removing all things that might provoke these spirits like leaving your lamp in the house and venturing into the dark.

**f) Not directly confronting the spirit using the usual instigative means.**

This is in part true, however, not descriptive of what a back door method really is. You might not directly confront the spirit at the house, but the 'back door' method is referring to what is done away from the premises that is haunted. Organizing prayer teams, having a mass said and gathering friends to pray a rosary etc. Instructing the household members to attend daily mass, and so forth…

**Which example best describes why Cold spots more commonly occur at a known haunted locations?**

    **a)    A Carrier brand "Heat pump" is removing the heat to 'cool' the room.**

Old school train of thought is that spirits use the heat in the room to manifest, as they can do with electrical energy. Evidence too often points to the contrary and the understanding of 'types' of spirits tells us about their traits and characteristic enough to say this isn't true.

    **b)    Ice cubes dropped in a fresh batch of Kool aid.**

A good analogy, they are ice cold, and the demonic presence affects the climate the more they manifest into the room(s). This is a matter of understanding how the room in a haunted location could become cooler, when all other natural reasons are exhausted. Like with the "Carrier Heat Pump" we find there is more than one way to heat (or cool) a home. In this case it is as simple as cold introduced to a warmer room with cool it down.

c) A drafty breeze coming up from the open cellar.

d) A fan blowing to cool a CPU on a computer

e) Winter chill coming from the north to cool the September heat.

f) All of the above

This is a question where the more true answer would be "all of the above, *except* answer "a)".


**What is meant by the term "Guns blazing" in the book?**

**a) Not taking your sweet time, during urgent the field investigation phases.**

Impatience is certainly not a virtue in this work it will be your worst and most dangerous impediment. You must take your time, try to be relaxed to better "take it all in". Pray for patience so that you will reflect a calmer demeanor and will be ready to wait for the right answer more easily. These things can't be rushed.

**b) A severe demonic attack.**

To answer this reply more briefly. "Guns blazing" isn't in a reference to the "enemy", or their strategy or behavior in any manner that applies to them.

**c) A "retaliation" or 'payback' from demonic spirits after an unsuccessful 'cleansing'**

The book quote reference is not to that of the would-be spirits with "Guns blazing".

**d) An early misuse of holy symbols, words, rituals.**

"Guns blazing" is saying try to access the situation before too quickly applying a possible solution. Mainly because if the person(s) affected are not adequately prepared, they will be the target of retaliation or "payback" for an unsuccessful deliverance.

**e) To always have a lot of faith by attending a lot of church services when you enter any supposed 'haunted location'.**

It is always helpful if your faith is deeply seeded in God the father, but as this spiritual/psychological war begins, it is only part of the armor and preparation(the most important part!). "Guns blazing" does not refer to the amount of faith one has.

## What are some common night attacks one might find as they try to sleep during the stage of "oppression"?

**a) Burning sensation from a phantom "touch".**

This is quite uncommon. The notion of "fire" is that in some thought, evil spirits linger in or have come from the fire world of "Hell". Though they bring their apparent "negative" traits, bringing fire and heat with them isn't all that common to experience. The sensation of cold is however more common, so an "ICY Touch" will be noted more often.

**b) Strangulation on the throat.**

Not as common as you might think. It is more widely accepted belief as the TV shows and movies telling their stories. Strangulation from a demonic spirit will occur without leaving marks as when a human hand does the dirty dead. Although we know of numerous cases where it did leave marks and they were photographed and within hours the marks were gone as if they never existed baffling and confusing the 'investigators'. Some oppressed will die in their sleep, as if by natural causes, when they died of this form of strangulation. Evidence of this attack, have rarely shown bruises, because the imprints on the neck would fade quickly over a few hours to a day. Spelling out that it is indeed "supernatural"

### c) A suffocating weight on their chest

This one is quite common experience, the sleep paralysis is consider a part of the attack, holding the victim still and all they can do is watch in terror as something emerges from the darkness and proceeds over the top of them in this manner.

### d) Induced heart attack

This may be brought about with one who has a weaker heart by simply frightening them to get their heart racing waking them up from a sound sleep. A very loud "Boom", a "Clang" glass breaking, or other sharp and loud phantom sounds that are quite disturbing in the night can really be shocking to the unsuspecting sleeper. On other occasion they can simply reach in and induce a heart attack. How effective they can be in this direct manner depends on the person and their level of faith and protection as well as the strength and magnitude of the demon(s) represented.

### e) A 'Life' force energy "feeding"

It is said "A suffocating weigh on their chest", is accompanied with a lack of energy the following days. So the two attacks are often related.

### f) Stabbing sensation on the body.

A sharp pin, not as commonly as feeling like knife, and the victim may have experienced this in their sleep. Getting disrupted from a deep sleep, which may or may not show bruises in the area can be quite disturbing. As we observe an experience involving pain or injury induced by "unseen hands" the more paranormal aspect is when there is no mark, yet there should be or bite marks, scratches or bruises heal up far too quickly.

**g)   A 'slap'.**

Some have been awoken by a slap, I wondered after hearing the description if it was a good way to awaken, although rudely, the person(s) so they were aware of what was in their room. A slap isn't always something of an 'attack' or from an 'evil' source.

**h)   A poke in the eye**

Choice "f", "g", and "h" are about equal in how common they might be, they favor the left eye and it can be quite painful as if a needed had penetrated the eye.
  Deborah Johnson (original name Glatzel, re: Devil in Connecticut case) experienced this, as did Denice Jones and Carmen Reed. (noteworthy "haunted" cases with more notoriety and media coverage.)

Comments:
As Hollywood sensationalizes supposed "True ghost" stories, some find this enough motivation to fabricate or exaggerate experiences told to field investigator. The

Catholic Church is very aware of this, and hence the "red tape" is to help avoid these individuals. It is very common and sometimes the doors can be closed even before the story is told. Again as with simple and common paranormal experiences, the client may be misrepresenting the truth, (in the least) as the stories lean to the more rare occurrences in the described details of their experiences. We might begin to suspect the truth is not being told from this.

## As outlined in my book, what are the five basic steps to deliverance?

### 1) Contrition

Truly sorry for your sins, make your piece with God and your supposed enemies, in the least in prayers for them.

### 2) Breaking attachments and Curses.

To break those things that might have given Satan a foothold and consecrate all to Jesus.

### 3) Environmental/Life choices and changes

All things that may offend God, some are more obvious, such as occult items, pornography, murder, idolatry hence the biblical quote:
*"If thy eye offend thee, pluck it out",* which really means to remove things and people from your life that are occasions (temptations) for sin.

4) **Words and Actions to Rebuke spirits**

Just as actions and words brought them into your life, by someone past or more recent the same can get it out. It is time to invoke the power of heaven to counter.

**5) Prevention**

"An ounce of prevention" is true, however, it is far easier to be 're-infected" by these entities after the first time, that it would have been before. So the same measure of prevention will be much more for the ones who have lived in a haunted home, or one whom was affected through possession. Sort of like patching a hole in a dam with bubble gum or mended broken bone with a scarf. This will remain a 'potential' weak point that will be tested with a variety tempting factors until you can no longer be tempted or simply fall into your temptation further. Prevention is a daily practice for life, once you have been infected/affected by these spirits on these higher levels.

**How might a Demonic spirit more commonly first enter your living space, check all that commonly apply:**

a) Through the walls
b) Ceiling
c) Floor (x = a correct choice)
d) Doorway (x)

e) **Window (x)**
f) **Portal (x)**

This question is often asked by the ones not seeming "New Agey" or with a "scientific" point of view. Does there really need to be an entry point like a portal for them to enter into your spiritual energy? Looking at commonly believed practices like that of an occultist attempting to make an opening using an inverted pentagram to allow a demon to enter this world as to do their bidding. One could say this was done through a ritual creating a "Portal" or a doorway between our world and theirs. A suicide can make a certain spot active, it doesn't mean a horde of evil spirits all flock in a inter-dimensional door way that needs to be forced shut to stop suppose paranormal ghostly activity. In truth I feel the existence of such hot spots, do not need to be specifically addressed and seem to confuse us as to the real problems (and solutions) at hand. We need to focus on the occupants of a house. Although I agree some areas might be more affected, labeling it a "portal" seems to over dramatize it in the very least.

Comments: Remember, that we are talking its first entry (appearance), not how it comes and goes afterwards.

## A Curse will not affect a "Christian" (T/F)

In an perfect world, where all those who are baptized "Christian" in any denomination and who consider themselves to be an observant "Christian" this statement might be true. These people would actually have devoted their daily living to Jesus, closely following the commandments and wouldn't be straying in and out of sinful practices. If this could be an accurate case scenario, this statement might be true. This is a very "gray" area, and this statement should Not be made without additional details. We do not mislead anyone into thinking they are "nuts" because they can't possibly be "possessed" or cursed since they are 'good Christians'. That is absurd and a bit "prideful", when some believe themselves to be so "bullet proof". Always draw that line between the two extremes, where those might have this belief, or they might believe every case of an "obsessive" self indulgent act means "possession" such as chain smoking, gambling or a drinking problem. We have seen people physically change after a deliverance session. Sometimes it is hard to say if the session simply helped them to get closer to God or if they did in fact have a demons influence miraculously removed by God and suddenly found they were no longer a slave to a cigarette for example. Keep an open mind on that. Do understand this is NOT possession, just more affected level of "demonization" and 'spirits of temptation' we all face one way or another throughout our lives.

**Curses are only the result of "Black Magic" (T/F)**

A "curse" is essentially carried out by a demon and sometimes given from the mouth of another human. Any demonic "attachment" or "mission" is considered to be a curse. When it comes from a person it is usually in order to carry out specific task in a dirty deed of revenge. Even supposed good some white magicians might send one to you that will have that negative entity affect you beyond and after the initial task is done. Lets take for example; a neighbor does you a favor and helps you get a job by doing a little "white spell", you get the job and beat the odds over other qualified applicants. Soon after the job begins, what some consider to be "bad luck" or a "series of unfortunate events" begin to take place. An uncanny amount of car repairs, your relationships suffer and start to breakdown, you lose valuable articles or misplace them frequently. The carried out task now has the linger affects of the dark spirit who support to have helped to turn the tide into your favor to help you get the job. Supposed "well wishes" might be better followed with a "Breaking curses prayer", in the same manner as if you had "ill wishes" or a direct curse placed upon you.

Think of it this way, they send a pizza guy who delivers to piping hot and fresh combos. They he proceeds to take off his shoes and socks and flops own on the couch. You ask him "What are you doing?", he ignores you and proceeds to eat all of your food, steals you cash, ransacks your house while you are at work then to add insult to injury he burns your house down. Now just imagine if this person was 'unseen' that had that accompanied the 'supposed' good with that 'free' pizza. There is no such thing as 'white' or 'good' magic, there is a very good reason to stay away from these occult practices.

**A Curse CAN NOT be broken unless you know the spell that has been cast. (T/F)**

To some extent this can be true, but most often NOT. An object will need to be uncovered in some cases that will affect the spell or curse. It will be better to find it and destroy it in the proper manner. Or the direct source of the curse must be brought to light and offered up to Christ. You must investigate by thinking on who might have access to your home or personal effects at work? If it is possible that you suspect someone might have had temporary access, check around the house. In what room do you feel the most affected? Is there an area that is more specific to activity and occurrences? Do you only have the nightmares when you doze off on the couch? In this you will try to localize a search. Where to look? More your personal space, if it is your room you suspect check under the mattress, and the bed and even INSIDE the mattress, in this I mean look for an anomaly where a careful incision could have been made as to slip in a better conceal the unholy object. I am not saying tear the mattress up, but be aware how cleaver these things can be concealed. Exorcist Fr. Gabriel Amorth told a story of how in a pillow the items that affected the individual were hidden from view.

Now start looking behind family portraits of photos on your wall. Look behind them, remove the inserted back covers if they can be removed easily, check for unholy symbols, tape artifacts stuck on the back. One person found a ribbon tied around a small piece of parchment which had the curse written on it. Don't rule out clothes either. But they will try to get it into something that will stay there longer and you will be more in close proximity to it more often.

GET Outdoors. Sometimes they will bury something in your yard, in the same manner that we might do a "four corners" blessing burning Sacramental. One might use the same thing to curse your property and those in it. Do or redo your four corners blessing, I am not sure you will find to easily the items they buried, even with a metal detector. A 'nail' with (chicken?) blood was included in one discover buried treasure left by some practitioner of Voodoo and this was only discovered by chance. The property owner wasn't even aware they should look for such a thing.

**Curses" are in essence" a "demonic attachment" (T/F)**

Refer to earlier in this book for a detail explanation....

**Pagans can not break a curse with "Christian" solutions. (T/F)**

Let me provide you with a meter of faith, consider "zero" position to be a someone such as Jeffrey Dahmer, while the position reading "100" to be one who is a Saint. All of us fall into between there somewhere, essentially for anyone, the higher the meter reads the more you are open to intercession from God and heaven.

We can never state that just because someone is a 'pagan', God in no way will listen to or answer their call. The fact is they may follow through with something that is considered a Christian based solution is reason enough at times to provide intercessory prayer and assistance. This is another case where we as humans should not and must not judge another. We cannot see the purity or ability of their soul to seek God nor can we know in advance how our prayers or assistance may affect their lives. NEVER assume just because they are of another faith or 'no' faith or not baptized into the Christian faith that God will not intercede if we call on him crying out to him from the sincerity and depths of our hearts and souls. You just may save another soul instead of turning another over to the dark side. Consider this passage in scripture MT 15:21-28 where Jesus rebuked a 'Canaanite' woman who needed help crying out "have pity me, Lord son of David! My daughter is tormented by a demon. He did not say a word in answer to her. The disciples came to Jesus and asked him "send her away for she keeps calling out after us". He said in reply "I was sent only to the lost sheep of the house of Israel". But the woman came to him and did him homage saying, "Lord, help me". He said in reply, "it is not right to take the food of the children and throw it to the dogs." She said "please Lord, even the dogs eat the scraps that fall from the tables of their masters." Then Jesus said to her in reply, "O woman, great is your faith! Let it be done as you wish." And her daughter was healed from that hour." Does this not remind us how we are to act Christ like?

We must remember that what God allows is a variable to his greater glory and for the good of souls.

## If you don't "Believe" in the curse, it will not affect you! (T/F)

Having a certain 'FAITH' in the effects of a curse and how it is going to directly affect you at some point is a form of psychological warfare. You can say "fear' is the opposite' of faith and placing a certain trust in a curse and having a fear of it, is giving it a certain power, whereas you should trust God alone. Again here opposites can cancel each other out. Having said that, now I will extend this line of discussion further as I said it may have "Some" affect. It doesn't matter if you believe it or not, you can be ignorant of the affects of cancer or diabetes and it will STILL AFFECT YOU. This is the same way its methods will not be obvious. How much it affects you will depend again on variables like Piety, uncommon grace and a willingness to let go and trust God . How you live you life and one of faith.

## OUIJA BOARDS – What of the following is True? Check all that apply:

**a) Ouija boards are not in themselves unholy, just a piece of word with a printed letters.**

Think of purpose and the invention of a 'thing'. Now think of what an Ouija board is used for it is by default more than the materials it is made from. There are enough demons to dispatch one demon to manipulate the board and the user for every board on the store shelves and in someone's closet. So the board already has a sort of demonic "attachment" that comes with the board, to try and help you by better pretending to be the entity you would want them to be. So many are deluded into thinking these are nice or benign spirits. They are not. They have the ability to make you think they are anyone *you* want them to be. For a lonely teenage girl: A boy who died tragically when he was a teen; Sci-Fi freaks, a "UFO Alien" or an "Inter-dimensional traveler". None of these 'intended' spirit boards are good. Using an angel board, an arch angel or you own "guardian angel", morning the loss of your son? They can mimic your dearly departed loved one to where you won't know you are being duped. That is their job and they've got years of practice.

**b) If a spirit is misspelling words, it is a "demonic" spirit.**

Words being misspelled don't tell us anything. We can't even assume it means the spirit isn't good with the

English language or even flunked out in spelling when in grammar school. It may however be part of the 'manipulation' to leave a puzzle of incomplete words, to peak your curiosity to play with 'it' more, to convey 'bad spelling' as to make you believe it is a child or as of many other deceptions it can come up with. Whatever the reason no 'good' or 'helpful' spirits talk on the board so we don't care if they can spell "*Supercalifragilisticexpialidocious*", a word I had to look up online to spell correctly. It doesn't mean anything that will help us solve the haunting.

### c) Both Human and Inhuman spirits will communicate through the board.

Seriously? I think everyone can agree on this one, but we have to note the 'Type' of spirit, or rather the nature of the spirit, whether it is human or inhuman, will be "evil" even if this is not clear by how it presents itself, look at the big picture and which side this supposed human spirit will be on with the demonic.

### d) ...It CAN be used safely in helping determine a spirit IS present at a location.

Everyone can also agree that there is a major risk for anyone to use the board. Where we can't agree is that there is no safe way to use the board period that will ensure absolutely no affects from the "dark ones".

**In the book, by "rebirth" I am referring to:**

**a) To discover your past life self through regression therapy.**

The keywords: "past self" and "regression therapy" is in support of long held Buddhist notion of 'reincarnation'. I am not referring to some 'rebirth' as in a spiritual sense, or into a new body or another animal body.

**b) To become a "Born again Christian".**
Does not apply at all .

**c) To experience an NDE (near death experience)**

Close, but no 'cigar', the near death experience itself is not what I am specifically referring to as "rebirth"

**d) A Human Ghost that is aware that it is a Ghost**

Not possible to our experience. Being so self aware as a disembodied spirit of some human ghost isn't a rebirth by any means.

**e) When a Human ghost is found possessing a living person.**

We have heard such horror from demons and their minions, who delight in being in the flesh of the human body. "To breathe " is more of a desire said to be from these spirits in a Hollywood flick, what they really seek is human 'warmth', which is shelter from where they came from where it seems to be too hot, humid or too cold. Comfort, relief, 'pleasure' which counter the discomforts they are known to feel. They also seem to desire the 'sins of the flesh' blurting out vile and disgusting words, with gestures and actions. Such a lust for human life that they can never fully have nor experience, their jealousy of the 'man' made by God is so strong and bitter it drives them.

**f) To die temporarily, "Flat-lining", and to survive that ordeal.**

This is what I am alluding to, you were "dead", even if for a short time. When you awaken your life might change for the better or worse spiritually. No one goes through this experience unchanged. Why is this? Mainly because one or more of the following; with #1 a 'hidden' and seldom realized fact.

1) Bringing back spirit attachments. - Get baptized AGAIN if you suspect this, ASAP!
2) Changes to the brain, 'dead zones' from loss of oxygen to the brain.
3) True, and NDE experience, even if they don't remember what it entailed might affect them spiritually afterwards.
4) But again, they may not even remember it!

## "Red eyes" are more often characteristic of:

Here we ask about "glowing" red eyes and not bloodshot eyes for example.

### a) An animal spirit

Not the spirit of an animal, although some will reflect a reddish color when you shine a light into their eyes at certain distances.

### b) Possessed victim

Black eyes is more the look, white eyes, the eyes might become 'red' from stress, a degradation of health, and so forth, "irritation" but not really "glowing red", which again might be more a Hollywood over dramatization thing.

### c) A demon of the "Black arts"

This is so often true that it is an indication that someone currently or previously living at the home has at some point dabbled in the black arts (satanism, witchcraft). Recent witnessed accounts of this type of spirit are more than likely telltale of someone currently dabbling in these occult practices. Use this info as a sort of inside look, and compare it with client testimony, they're often not forthcoming in telling you this. I think they'll suspect it in this case, their actions through the occult dabbling is a prime reason and motivation for the haunting.

### d) Condemned Human spirits

Too rare to even mention here, the answer of [c] is the most correct and although it's form might better compare to a black shadowy robed figure, a similar demon might appear as an animal or human.

### e) None of the above

**A human spirit can not possess a person... Circle all statements that are "true")**

### a) Without the aid of a demonic spirit...

There is a certain lack of the knowledge and wisdom as well as the "power' for a human spirit to alone possess a human.

### b) ...Alone.

Applies to number one, you might as well let your dog into your car and say "DRIVE!"

### c) The can "inhabit", but not "possess"

Under the term possession, since they are limited in their control and do not do it alone, this applies.

d)   They can not "control" the person

Sometimes they have spoken through the possessed, if the mouth moves in sync to this 'other' voice, this is a control of the mouth.

e)   **None of the above**

The key here is a human spirit may be along for the "joy ride" but is not really the 'one' possessing the person. To "possess" as we should understand it doesn't mean alone to "inhabit". There is also confusion as to an attachment and a possession. An attachment can speak through someone while they are under hypnosis and it isn't possession because when they awake, there is no longer that connection.

**Lucifer is... (check all that apply)**

a)   A 'fallen angel'
b)   The highest ranking devil
c)   The one called "satan" in the bible and by other references.
d)   The dragon from the apocalypse.
e)   The "Advocate"
f)   The "Light bearer"
g)   The "lord of the flies"
h)   The prince of darkness

Beelzebub is the "Lord of the flies".
The "Advocate" is the opposite to his nature.

**A client tells of a "shadowy being" that is scaring the kids, sometime witnessed at 'night' and 'daytime' as well, and it also witnessed by the parents. Based on this information alone what might you advise?**

**a) Do not advise until you get more information.**

We can offer advice that will help them to play it safe.

**b) Inform them, "They have a demon", and that you will be taking measures to help them.**

There are red flags here to say it could be a 'demon', and to recommend that it would be treated as such. But approaching the family with this information is possibly harmful other than just recommending solutions that apply to a "type: Evil Inhuman Spirit". We should *avoid* the word demon initially, and if you pass them prayers that mention a rebuke of "The devil and his minions" you can tell them it is to be better safe than sorry", especially if the person lives alone. They are far more psychologically affected when they live alone.

**c) Give them prayers to say, send Saint Benedict Medals for the family to wear.**

Anytime I hear of 'shadows' witnessed clearly by more than one person especially, I suggest that you get them 'protection' ASAP that includes prayers they can say and any form of 'religious' medals they will accept to place their faith in for protection around their house.

**d) Tell them to try smudging the place with a "sage stick."**

Sage is a Native American practice, and alone will *not* be effective against evil. Our Native American friends don't use 'sage' to confront and expel 'demonic spirits'. If anything at all, it may amuse them and entice them to play with you. If you are a follower of the 'ghost/demon' busting enthusiasts of the prime time television dramas and attempt to use 'sage' on any spiritual entity, the reality is likely they will lay low to give an illusion it is working to further confuse those affected by their presence.

**e) Tell them since they are "Christian" and believe in "Jesus" they have nothing to fear.**

I wish I could say it was this simple and a true statement. People have had bibles ripped out of their hands, or had it thrown at their hands. "Now what"? It is dumbfounding to some with fundamental beliefs.

**f) Tell them to ignore it and see if it goes away**

You should never ignore it, in the least pray silently behind the scenes while family and those affected are perhaps reassured to avoid the group 'fear factor". That can only go for so long and this advice depends on the level of activity and stage of the haunting.

**A client tells you their child is "seeing ghosts", she makes mention that the child is a "sensitive". Based on this info alone, what would you reply with next?**

**a)   Do not advise until you get more information.**

This can be a good solution and is better than most of the other answers below. But this is really ignoring what you have just learned until you get more information. Which is not good either.

**b)   Inform them, "The child has a demon", and that you will be taking measures to help them.**

Too soon to jump to such conclusion, why get them afraid at all and use the "D" word when you haven't even investigated?

**c)   A family curse is in play**

This is the best bet solution but without more information it is good advice even for starters.

### d) The child is gifted.

A home blessing is a good practice that should be done regardless and every so often. However for this situation it can be a bit premature, not exactly sure what you are dealing with there, as we haven't even determined it is warranted and least we forget about "shaking the bee hive" of demons. Again, DON'T USE SAGE. Use blessed Frankincense and Myrrh if you are going to smudge and bless a house.

### e) Tell them since they are Christian and believe in Jesus they have nothing to fear.

This is more of that notion that somehow being a "born again" Christian makes you and your family an impenetrable fortress. Also, a mere "belief" in Jesus is not enough, how do their do acts of faith show in their thoughts, words and actions? This is what really says they are Christians?

We should always assume that just because they are Christians doesn't exclude them from any sort of haunting or possession. In fact it may make them more likely since being Christian can provoke these dark entities.

### f) Advise them to 'just ignore it' and see if it goes away.

### g) Aliens might have been seen in your area advise the child not to talk to it.

h)     None of the above apply

i)     All of the above apply

Because of what I went through in 2010, with my book contents on trial for my children's custody, I choose to not address this beyond the correct answer note.

**In the book, what do I mean by "shaking the beehive"? (Check all that apply)**

**a)   Taking action to rebuke evil spirits, therefore drawing retaliation.**

This can happen on more than one level. Even exposed holy symbols can set a demon on to a retaliatory course. Even if it is later that's same night.

**b)     Anytime you begin an "exorcism" or cleansing**

We have to remember that when we start any action that might stir up the infesting spirits, it will likely draw some retaliation. So if it is done to soon, it will endanger others unnecessarily.

**c)    Provoking the spirits.**

With answers [a] and [b] for examples, this is provoking whether it is your intention or not. As provoking can be done in more discreet matters, such as simple questions "is anyone here" that is still by definition 'provoking', but clearly not "shaking a beehive". This selection does not apply.

### d) Confronting the spirits directly

This is in no way related; it may not necessarily provoke or draw a retaliation to confront directly. This can be a matter of shouting "what do you want"?

### e) Insulting the spirit as to get evidence.

Insulting the spirit might stir things up, as disrespecting the proud demonic can draw retaliation. But shaking the beehive is more in your methods from investigation on through deliverance. There is nothing more fool hardy and TV show style, cowboy recklessness as this. This does not apply.

Comments:
Typically, we want o avoid some form of religious provocation in any form, even exposed crucifixes, you might wear around your neck.

**Complete this sentence; A Home "blessing"...**

### a) Should always be done by properly ordained "Clergy". See the NEXT PAGE for exceptions

**b)   Can be done by the home owners, when a priest is not available.**

The home owners have a certain authority over their property that only a more pious person of God could supersede. (Their level of faith and piety applies)
Bless your house and property, even when you don't think it needs it. (An once of prevention)

**c)   Should be done with caution**

Good advice, we always want to assess the situation as to the what level a demonic presence is evident, then to better know if they can respond to any measures a blessing or a deliverance method, with some form of physical retaliation. Everyone involved in the blessing should follow up with a protection prayer to help break the affects and possible 'payback' a demonic spirit might deliver. No one can be right 100% of the time, as these things can happen, but we avoid them at all cost. In this it would be one of those cases where the demonic was simply laying low. And you just woke up the sleeping giant. This is why many of us are jittery at yet another one who will surface as a supposed "demonologist", because it takes a great deal of knowledge and understanding, plus a certain level of discernment that can only come from God. To make a good call as to when to proceed safely with a blessing or a deliverance we must do thorough investigative work, assess from all angles and only then proceed with caution on a possible solution. We don't want the family for example, to pay the big price for our mistakes in incorrectly indentifying the seriousness of a demonic haunting.

**d) Is to rebuke evil spirits**

It is not designed to rebuke evil spirits, but to bless or imbue the environment with God's positive grace or 'energy'. This might have an effect to run of some lower level evil spirits, but it is not specific to the point of a 'blessing'. It is a good practice to perform a blessing after each successful exorcism, or deliverance, for sometime after to keep the environment more 'positive' with God's grace. This will help ensure that the demonic forces will not return.

**e) Should be done at night when the spirits are there.**

Why wait until they are at full power? There is nothing to gain by waiting, on the contrary better to take advantage of the daylight hours while you can.


**What is more common reason for a 9 year old to "see ghosts"?**

**a) Via Hereditary "divine spirits"**

Remember that a baptism originally is more than a mere 'christening' or 'anointing' it is a simple exorcism that will help break some generational ties via the family tree. More importantly it is a covenant with God that professes his authority and decries any satan may have to truly give the child a 'fresh start'.

**b)     God has bestowed gifts onto the child**

Likely no, supposed gifts wouldn't show up so early, but it can happen, curse and hereditary demonic can affect them immediately with notable special abilities, and supernatural occurrences that surround them. Always quietly suspect a 'negative origin' first, pray about it, baptism ASAP, later religious retreats, etc. As so if it is in fact anything negative behind it, it will weed them out. Padre Pio was gifted since before he could attend public school and it is rare.

**c)    A Family curse**

This is as with choice 'A', as in a generational - hereditary demonic affect. A Catholic Baptism can nullify such a curse usually, and prayers to break it further. One often becomes a "Sensitive" (psychic or medium) when oppressed or possessed by evil spirit(s). (such as the divine spirit in acts 16:16). So we consider any supposed "gift" first to maybe come form the dark side first, before it is assume some gift from God. To better play it safe.

### d) The child is living in a demonic infestation

Once you have lived through the affects of a demonic infestation, you will never be the same. You sensitive side can be heightened from I believe is as so you can better be ware when they dark ones come calling.

Both Deborah Johnson and her brother Alan Glatzel for example, (The Devil in Connecticut), became somewhat more 'sensitive' after their ordeal. I feel this was as so they can better watch their backs. It is a matter of defense, so we can better detect their

'return', and to be more sensitive to their presence. Others will say when they know you are aware of their existence on a higher level, they don't so discreetly sneak around as they did before.

### e) Child is chronically ill

The drugs they might take could open them up as I warn of how drugs can make you sensitive and more vulnerable. Sometimes, if the child is past the "age of reason", the spirit may be trying to sway the child in what little time they have. Third, this could be an affect from brain damage related to this illness, such as when I describe how head trauma and near death experiences can alter affect a part of the brain that otherwise would be purposely subdued by wizards with [certain drugs] as so they can see the demons they will manipulate through spells.

**f)     The child is not (properly) blessed/baptized**

Generational demons will affect the child, which might include their past sins. Again this is an older Christian belief as many that are still understood in the Catholic-Orthodoxy faith.

**g)     Child has had a head injury.**

Refer to the point I make in Selection [e] about the child's 'illnesses.

**h)     None of the Above can be true**

**i)     Any one of the above could be true**


**What is likely the real reason lights may dim when a demonic spirit enters a lit room? (check all that may apply)**

**a)     To frighten you**

There is something to gain by helping you away from "faith" and into "fear", fear must be defeated when you work in these cases, pray often o conquer this enemy within you! As it will be used against you!

**b) They are feeding on the energy source that powers the lights.**

An old parapsychology notion, demons do not need electrical energy, they more gain strength from your weaknesses and permission by your sinful shortcomings which gives them access. Heat and Electrical is of no use to them.

**c) They truly advert to light, and are diming the lights for a certain 'comfort'.**

This statement is the most true, but they do rely on our fear of the dark, not just their power within in.

**d) Their negative energy is countering the electrical source, thus canceling it out to some degree.**

The proof is another theory, a more metaphysical or spiritual answer should be considered first, before one of science. After all we are dealing with "spiritual beings".

**A client calls you to update you on recent 'activity', and makes mention that two days ago, at about 12:30AM, a black haired spirit appeared at her bedside, it was an old woman with 'white eyes' it said:**
**"Your God can't help you now", screamed as it turned into an appearance of a rotting corpse and it**

disappeared. You suspect, the story is not in the least all true. Why?

**a) The spirit did NOT appear closer to 3AM, as an evil spirit would do normally.**

In early stages of infestation a two hours span after 2am is a more likely time for a "visitor", this is consider, but not the most relevant piece of information to make the investigator suspicious.

**b)   White eyes are not so common and are rare.**

Yes, this is *NOT* a common description in true encounters and is a 'red flag' for an interviewer.

**c)   She waited two days before telling about something like this.**

When something this horrific occurs they will call you THAT SAME NIGHT, usually within minutes right after this occurs. This can be the most significant trait of one who is exaggerating or fabricating stories. This is not normal for one who might experience such a thing in real life.

Listen to how they talk about it also, are they calm? Does their voice quiver or sound desperate or afraid?

**d) "Your God can't help you now", is a movie quote.**

Yes it is, movies fuel the imagination and the delusion or attention seeker. Whatever the motivation, Hollywood gives some false notions about haunted houses and spiritual warfare itself, and the repeat what this seem as a true experience this can be a red flag.

**e) It is uncommon for apparitions to change appearance into something like a corpse or rare for a spirit to reveal itself as such.**

Most true encounters don't entail this as "white eyes" are not characteristic of the ghost or demons, Hollywood finds white eyes to be "creepy", so- it likes to use it again and again in ghost stories for the better drama.

**All human ghosts in that phase of existence Catholics call "purgatory" would not be able to speak, if they appear to you. (T/F)**

It is more common that they would not speak if it is an apparition; however there is nothing that say they can not. One person cited Father Gabriel Amorth almost in saying this is absolute that they will not be able to speak. This quoting father Amorth might be from his observation of cases he worked on. We also must remember that Fr. Amorth is an "Exorcist", dealing more with people than places, which is very clear when you read his books. And a ghost haunting so not something an exorcist is going to deal with. Second he is Italian and that is his primary language some translation errors might have taken Father Gabriel Amorth out of context. Such as in one section:

*"any spirits procured at séances are demons and any ghosts or poltergeists are actually demons, when people die their souls go straight to heaven or purgatory, They don't roam the earth."*

**Then in another paragraph he states elsewhere:**

*"...there sometimes appears a third type of phenomenon, distinct from the other two: ghosts. Ghosts are apparitions of people who are in Purgatory. These apparitions have characteristics which are always the same and very different from infestations"*

Keep in mind also the book wasn't likely checked for accuracy, it is for all of us to catch occasional mistakes in the may we might state something. Just as you the reader may also find in my book. This is why I say, feel free to e-mail me and ask me to elaborate something that I have written, be sure to point to exactly (the page and paragraph) in what you are referring to so I can be looking at the same statement where I can better clarify.

**Poltergeist cases are more often "PK energy" related to an adolescent. (T/F)**

I highly doubt this can be otherwise but rarely if ever true. Demonic have a "coming out party" and the sexual energy from the person gives even the lower ranks some power to manifest, even if it is but a short time. These cases will more often cease as mysteriously as they began when the child makes a change or action that either appeases them or rebukes them. Such as proceeding with confirmation, or a negative swing, phones mysteriously ringing is quite common too.


**Demons can not hurt you if you are not afraid of them. (T/F)**

This is an older myth, but luckily not as popular as it was even 10 years ago. The sensationalism of TV shows, although have it's extreme negative impact, also makes people ware of demonic activity on a higher level than to used to understand these topics sometime ago.


**Christians can be hurt by demons even with "faith" (T/F)**

A counter statement of answer this as correct, inline with the notion that is foolhardy to believe that Christians are somehow bulletproof because they are

"Born again" in Christ. Which is has too many grey areas to say such a simple statement can be true.

## The Catholic Church teaches all suicides go to hell. (T/F)

Your parish minister or priest might lead you to believe this, but is this what they are really saying? This is not a Catholic /Orthodox belief in its origin, but a result form bible only (solo scriptura) fundamentalists, not fact. Only God knows who might actually go to hell after death, it is not ours to judge. We do however pray for their soul to ensure they do escape such a fate.

## A pact with Satan can not be broken...

### a) If the person dies...

It might be broken in that it is 'fulfilled', however, only God knows if such a pact can be bound in the afterlife. This depends on the person and other variables such as though who might offer prayer and penance on their behalf. The same as with any of the deceased. Another one which can vary to Gods will.

### b) If they are uncooperative

The steps to deliverance from such a pact will require thoughts words and deeds. From the heart a trustful surrender to Jesus. They must declare and vow against

Satan and what he has offered. Prayers must continue for life, even if they no longer feel oppressed.

Recitation of a simple prayer daily to reaffirm a commitment to God and his commandments and a rejection of Satan and his works.

### c) ...It cannot be broken, period!

Those in the Satanic church they want you to buy into this, or that you will die if you try to depart from the faith. Part of this is that YOU believe this and your belief is important, since it gives this pact, and the demonic spirits, FAITH. All spells can be broken, we just want to ensure the victim doesn't somehow die before her/her demonic attachments that resulted from the curse, are truly severed. When such evil is directed at you, you can't breathe easy in your life thinking you can begin to turn away from God again. These are the ravenous dogs awaiting for you to leave your home without an armed escort, which in reality is God's angels and Saints that might protect you, even as you sleep.

### d) Only by a Satanic rite to "undo" the pact.

Never use magic to counter affect 'magic' or 'curses' this is not even in the least use a 'positive' counter acts the 'negative' it is in expecting a "house divided against itself".

e) **Unless someone offers themselves in your place.**

This might be a notion that comes from the movie, "The Exorcist", a "Martyrdom' still might occur with one sacrificing their life for one afflicted with demonization. However, it is more as a causality of war (spiritual warfare), not ever some 'self-sacrifice' or 'suicide' pact. Such was the case when Arnie Johnson challenged the demon that was beating his Girlfriends kid brother. It is normal for us to become angry and say something to that affect:

*"Leave him alone, you bully he's just a kid! You want to fight someone you coward, then fight me!!"*

This is a self-less act but a foolish one, as a result Arne became possessed a short time later. This is almost similar to offering yourself for exchange, but as we know how this and all other story really go. There is never a switch, the boy continued to be affected. Such a thing would happen to those who might try to offer themselves in such a way. Or this could happen in any (occult) service apart from an "exorcism".

## What is a "Jinn" essentially?

a) **Beings of "fire"**

Fire is associated wrongly with demons, when artic cold better describes them. The fire or intense heat is based on a notion of Hells fire.

As we rarely find "heat spots" like "cold spot" can be felt. But, we find that seeing Fire maybe more of an indication of a purgatory human spirit. (along with other indications), or might even relate to an event that took place.

There are demons of fire, but they might work more discreetly in setting fires to work an accident, or as the late Ed Warren believed to be some of those unexplained cases of "spontaneous human combustion", can be a result from a demonic encounter.

**b)   A demon**

A demon by another other name is still s "demon" you can quote that.

**c)   A fable "Tales of the Arabian knights"**

Another fable based on Fact like the way Camelot, or King Arthur and his knights of the round table parallels, the biblical story of David. Vladimir Dracula, began with "Vlad' the impaler". The Arabian spin on this type of demon is what will vary.

**d)   Muslim Folklore, mythology**
See letter answer "c"

**e)   A for the "Genie" that grants you three wishes**

Related to the choice of 'c' and 'd', the Islamic "Jinn" is what we call a "Genie" in the states. We all remember the story of the cross roads? Wherein a blues guitarist whom attend his gift from a devil whom at first pretended to be a retired guitarist.

## What is the most common reason for a demon to return so soon after a successful exorcism?

**a)   The demon never left, it was simply 'lying low' for a time.**

This is more true for a haunted location and is not something so much more localize and confined as with a possession case.

**b)   The client became to falters from the prescribed prayers and daily practices.**

Sadly, this is more often true, typical human to resume life as usual after the 'ordeal'. But in reality you are tainted, and like a diabetic you can never go about your life eating and drinking, living as you did before.

**c)   A 'curse' is being repeated.**

If it is suspected the source of the demonic affliction is indeed a 'curse' that can individual who still maybe 'at odds' with the victim. This can very well happen. It is like being 're-infected' with a virus. Sometimes this maybe coming in contact with a cursed item or location on a second occasion.  If an object is again swallowed or hidden away undiscovered, that is part of the curse, this might make it a bit hard to get rid of, for the reasons I cite above, that being exposed to it time and time again,

Re-infects' for one reason, and second the object is better to be destroyed as to achieve better results and faster in breaking the curse.

If the proper measures are taken to break the curse in prayers for example, this only needs to be done in reality once. I always say to repeat these prayers for three days in 'honor of the holy trinity. Rather than to say them just once.

Have a priest bless you after wards. Catholics should go to make a 'good confession' and receive communion ASAP. The more done spiritually the better.

### d)   The deliverance was focused on the wrong person.

This can happen, but we won't see one person exhibit symptoms to hint they are 'possessed' while the truly afflicted person slips by without being noted. No real mistakes as such would be made, but the possessed might go undetected to a certain degree. Just look at serial Ted Bundy and how his neighbors thought he was a "Model Neighbor". This is what Malachi Martian referred to as "perfect possession', I prefer to call it more as a peaceful collaboration, a possession seem to be you are a "hostage" not collaborating with the enemy.

**e) They begin to resume a practice that was part of the reason they were affected by a demonic presence to begin with.**

This might occur in a variety of ways, and can be the main reason for it returning. In one case, a man began to do "psychic-readings" again, against advice, and this information was concealed from me. It came back, and much worse, it was apparent that he had done something to have what was quite a successful exorcism from an Anglican Priest, to return with a "vengeance". The indications were there, and I interviewed him and came up with nothing. Then a friend revealed what he was again doing behind the scenes, he started doing them again "because he needed the money", and shortly after his successful deliverance. In his case it wasn't merely some notion that 'Divination" is wrong for a Christian. It was more in it was determined that a spirit began communication to him, and he was merely curious, and this is what started the infection that lead to a form of possession at some point.

**f) The true source of the "demonization" was not directly dealt with.**

Methods that do not directly command the spirit to leave in the name of Jesus for example, might chip away at the affects of a possession or oppression and give some relief to the symptoms. But without a formal rebuke.

g) **Only one demon had been expelled, overlooking 'other' demons.**

Unless names and their numbers are known there is no real well to tell if a lone demon returns or one of it's minions are still there. We should assume in every case there is likely more than one evil spirit to rebuke.

**The more common reason an Incubus encounter will often begin because of...**

a) **A person at the household current or past residence lured it in, through some form of sexual perversion.**

See explanation for letter answer 'e'

b) **A practice of the dark arts.**

Some practices purposely call upon a sexual demon (or as they often believe as a 'god')

c) **Fantasies of a "Casanova lover"**

All sin begins with a mere thought and desire, which can turn to an obsession to where at some point you ignore what you know is wrong to satisfy this obsession.

**d) A type of "haunting" is already at the residence.**

This may be true that more than one of these choices may have been applicable to one who previously lived at your residence or slept on your bed, or worn those thrift store clothes, or driven your automobile. Be aware that buying used anything can hand down some of their attachments.

**e) The person already engaged in some of what the church considers to be "sinful sexuality"**

These immoral sins do invite and empower a specific demonic, one of lust. So when opportunity comes for an invitation, this type of demon is the first in line waiting at the door. This is why I say, if you hear of stories of a supposed spirit that is begin to molest (or worse), especially one member of the household. Consider that they are likely in need of spiritual help as well, as they have already appease this demon more than once through their thoughts words and actions of sinful sexuality.

**f) The victim does not take early measures to rebuke the spirit at its first signs.**

A late solution on most things that affect us, is Always a bad idea. A delay in fixing car brakes can be fatal, ignoring signs of high blood pressure can lead to a stroke. Take action early to "Nip it in the bud" before it blossoms to a much bigger problem.

The problem in this is, the sexual side is far to tempting to cut off, it is a sin appeasing the flesh and people often don't let it go all that easy. I say again, that the real war all begins within your spirit, in our free will.

**Why should holy oil or Holy Water be used over blessed salt?**

**a)    Salt is not a "sacramental"**

Neither is blessed wheat, this is a matter of something that is pure, when it is blessed.

**b)    Salt is a pagan practice, like throwing rice at weddings.**

Any non-Christian-Judeo usage of salt is likely derived from the old Judeo practice, or the simple fact that a pure element such as salt is a positive that can in itself affect evil at some level, just as with water.

**c)    It is better as a 'preventative' than for a 'cleansing'.**

Because of [e] below this can be true. Holy Water will dissipate fast, it doesn't linger, so will oil to a certain extent. But the residue will stay a while. Salt, it does dissolve from water, humidity, or some moisture, can last even longer. This lingering property might be the only benefit over water.

**d)     Salt is not easy to attain, as holy water, it is not 'free'**

True in part, you can't go to church and get it from a silver dispenser and table salt in general isn't "pure and natural".

**e)     It has corrosive properties**

This maybe the best reason to not use it. Salt will corrode metal, eats away at carpets. It can be quite a mess if you use it to bless an entire house and not just a room. I say use it across thresholds and window sills and it will also keep out bugs!

**Which of the following are NOT carried or worn for "protection" into a suspected demonic haunted location:**

**a)     Saint Michael medal**

A choice that doesn't provoke, and Michael is a protector, I am not aware of it's actual origins to say it is divinely inspired, and not just stuck as an honorarium, as the Holy face medal seems to be to the should of Turin.

### b) Saint Benedict Medal

One of the *best* choices.

### c) A Blessed Crucifix.

Worn on the outside or hung on the wall, is an known or unknown location that can be in the least potentially a demonic infestation. It is used for "religious provocation" and even by an exorcist in such a matter, in short exposing a crucifix in a haunted house can be a dangerous thing.

### d) Rosary Beads

As a rosary has a crucifix, attached to it, we might have it blessed, or pray with it often. But it in itself isn't a sacramental of protection.

### e) Sacred heart picture

Another that would help to provoke but not protect.

### f) Saint Christopher medal

The patron saint of travel, the model is of course said to be good to wear for "safe travels", not spiritual warfare.

g)    **Relic of Padre Pio**

Refer to 'e'

**Which of the above are not specifically used for daily protection? (enter all letters)**

Select letters d, e, f, and g.

**During an "Exorcism" a demon indentifies itself with the name of a known higher demon.**

a)    **The name might be to frighten the exorcist into thinking he is dealing with a more powerful demonic.**

As with all of these choices, we have to remember, that truth is not a boundary with the evil ones.

b)    **The demon may be identifying itself by it's hierarchy, not it's actual name.**

c)    **This is at least the name of one of the demons whom are affecting the possessed.**

d)    **All of the above -** > This choice is the most true.

e)    **None of the above** – An incorrect choice

**Finish this sentence, Objects... (check all that apply)**

a) **Can become possessed...**

It is referred to better as an "infestation", possession is having a certain part of your body hostage and under control of the demons that inhabit within. A 'dancing doll' might be animated by the demon but it is still merely "infested" with the spirit(s).

b) **All have an "aura".**

The aura from living things will energize objects, some more than others will hold this energy.

c) **Can be "infested"**

As I cite with selection [a], the statement is correct.

d) **Can be Exorcised**

Sometime it is better to destroy the object properly than to exorcise the demonic attached to, or infesting it. It has been done, think of a house as a large object. There is a risk as to where it will go after it is exorcised or destroyed. Which is why the proper prayers/rituals should be performed as to not just drive the spirit out, but to also send it to the proper place and bind it from affecting anyone else. Especially in some cases of retaliation, for example the owners of the object and those who might be present at the ritual.

**e)   Can be "cursed"**

Object that are purposely 'cursed' is quite common. We find that object that are supposed to bring good luck, will bring miss fortunes to another or only brought like to the original owner for a short time.

**f)   None of the above.**

This statement is the complete reverse of the actual correct answer.


**Based on the biblical passage ACTS _____, what can we validate this passage truly means?**

**a)   Pagans can not expect to ward off evil spirits by merely saying Jesus name.**

I can attest this is not true. And as one who follows the older Christian faith, we understand how Jesus name itself will affect evil sprits to some degree even if the name is spoken by a person who doesn't believe he is the son of God. It is the name itself alone.

**b) Only legitimately ordained clergy can exorcise demons in Jesus name.**

I recommend this, or course clergy will vary, and this stamen is very vague.

**c) Only Christians should expect to expel demons.**

To expel them, drive them out beyond methods of appeasement? I would say 'yes' this is more true
In selection [a] I make mention how saying Jesus name may wad off an evil spirit, to try to drive them away with authority using Jesus name can get mixed results. In part if the home owner commands the spirits to leave, as the owner in some cases they might be leaving. But not so easy in this alone. This is why we call for "intercession", have our heavenly 'positive' spirits escort these thugs out of our homes and out of our lives. Christians use Jesus name. Orthodox Christian/Catholics will add in intercession from the angels and Saints, which I feel is more effective.
The "advocates" as the saint can be will act on out behalf. Our heavenly father has placed his armies often at our disposal to some degree, but we have to pray for this and by Gods will and in Jesus name.

d) **Those of the Jewish faith can not use Jesus name to rebuke evil spirits.**

The same applies to pagan, oddly we find that those considered as 'pagan' are more open to the usage of the name of Jesus, than those of the Jewish faith. But I always would think we are closer to the Jewish faith than say the 'wiccan faith'. In this that is not that case.

**Lilith is essentially…**

a) **Entirely a Myth**

We suspect she is not entirely a myth. There are many stories of Lilith based on apocryphal documents both Latin and English versions later. This statement would be 'false'.

b.) **Was in fact Adams first wife.**

We find to many inconsistencies to say this is not true. Let me outline some main points:

The common 'historic' stories claim "Lilith' would not 'submit' to her mate Adam and preferred to be "on top". When we read the Genesis story to understand that Adam and Eve were like naive children before the tree of knowledge, the Lilith story contradicts this in saying that she did have carnal knowledge and was having intercourse with Adam before Eve was created for him from his own rib. During the Middle Ages, these stories were expanded upon in the Jewish tradition of the *'Midrashim'* and the mystical Jewish *'Zohar'* from Spain. These later texts describe Lilith in detail as she is listed as on of the *'Qliphoth'*, corresponding to the Sephirah Malkuth (Lowest place on the earthly plane) in the Kabbalistic 'Tree of Life'. The demon Lillith, the evil woman is described to be as a beautiful woman who transforms into a blue, butterfly-like demon and is associated with the power of seduction. In the Dead Sea Scrolls she is mentioned 19 times around 10BCE in the Songs for the Sage scrolls. Lillith is also said to appear in the 5c Latin Vulgate, translated in the book of Isaiah 34:14, Lillith is translated Lamia. Further speculation associates the Lamia/Lillith with a Greek goddess that was a half human half snake cannibalistic goddess. This she demon has associations in many other cultures as well. It appears that as you follow those lines of history, we have created in here, what our deepest darkest fears have associated her to be. History is interesting to say the very least.

### c)     Is the name of a succubus demon

This could be truer, and sex or 'female goddess' of any non-Christian-Judeo faith or belief system could very well be classified of the type of demons that are the incubi and succubus.

### d) Is a cat demon

There is no hint of this in any historical writings in relation to a feline reference.

### e) Is in the bible

The story is in an apocryphal text (see above b) 1.) I think as you explore Genesis it is pretty self explanatory. It is easy to debunk the Lilith theory on the time line of biblical events alone if you are considering the apostolic books we do have in both the Orthodox and the King James version of the bible. There was something very real in history that was representative of this 'she-demon', but the evidence is not clear where she came from or why she is even mentioned. Sadly there is a remaining 'romance' of Lillith in occult, wiccan and magical orders. She is worshipped like an idol and over dramatized. Dangerous.

## Religious provocation is NOT necessarily done to:

### a) To attain information needed prior to the full Exorcism (Roman Ritual)

Sometimes, it lays low in the presence of those whom try to validate a "presence" in the least. And such action must be done because this "hiding" by the enemy is an ongoing occurrence, and will stall any real help that would be needed from Clerical help or an authorized Roman Catholic Exorcism.

**b) To force an evidence capture, EVP, Video, or Photographic.**

This is to say that after it is forced out of hiding, it still can be captured my some form of media, and not just witnessed. We should rely more on witnesses, and not camera, video, Audio recordings, which they can so well still elude, even when your own ears and eyes, sense can detect them. Try to not seek a prize, but needed proof for the right people only; NOT THE PRESS AND MEDIA.

**c) To weaken the spirit prior to deliverance.**

If anything it enraging it, this is why only an ordained Exorcist should do this provocation.

**d) To force the spirit to reveal its presence.**

This is what Religious provocation is, the purpose more is to reveal what is hiding or unknown. So this is not the correct choice.

**e) - None of the above**

**Which object or holy symbol will NOT alone have an affect on this demonic if unblessed:**

**a)** **Pure sea salt**

Consider the purity of sea salt… Read on…

**b)** **A bare "cross"**

Straight off mold or workshop bench, as a plain cross, it really has virtually no affect. Except in how it might help to give the one whom holds it a faith. It is more a symbol for Christians, but the crucifix is the true sign of Jesus' victory of sin and death, which makes the devil howl in pain.

**c)** **Pure water**

The more pure elements, as with sea salt, are a good starting point.

**d)** **A crucifix**

Does not apply to the question

**e)** **A Saint Benedict Medal**

Because of its inspiration and significance to honoring Saint Benedict it has the power to protect. It is better than say a plain cross.

### f) Frankincense and Myrrh

Some scents seems to lure, other repel. Alone this seems to have a quality the evil ones don't like. As with the more pure elements of water and sea salt, again here, even unblessed.

## What of the following was NOT divinely inspired?

### a) Saint Benedict Medal
The books themselves are not the medal.

### b) Saint Michael medal

Does not have origins based on divine inspiration, although it honors Saint Michael, and the iconic statue. But the medal itself was not inspired as the rosary and St. Benedict Medal for example. This medal is more of an "honorary medal".

### c) "Holy face" medal

This honors the 'Shroud of Turin' as a true relic of the face of our living Lord Jesus Christ. But not divinely inspired.

### d) The Rosary

The rosary is a form of combined prayer and meditation that has been around for over 1200 years. The origin of the rosary dates back to the ninth century where Irish monks would recite and chant the 150 Psalms of the bible as a major part of their worship. The people were drawn to the beauty of this form of worship but it was very difficult to learn all the Psalms and they weren't written copies available. The innovated version (Rosarium) was widely spread by the Blessed Alan de la Roche of the Dominican order of Monks containing 50 prayers as opposed to the 150. The prayers of this Rosarium were later broken out into sets of two and these groupings became known as decades. The rosary we know today is the result of many changes dating back several hundred years. Countless interventions still occur today and the power of divine graces the rosary offers are available to everyone who is willing to give it a chance. So legend has it has it that our 'Rosarium" was presented by the blessed Mother to St Dominic. Thus being it is considered to be divinely inspired. This to is another Catholic practice although many other religions use 'prayer beads' to keep track of prayers said.

e) **Scapular**

The word Scapular comes from the word *'scapulae'* which is Latin for shoulders. As used today it refers to two specific Christian sacramental, namely the monastic and the devotional scapulars. The Monastic originated around 7the century in the Order of St Benedict. The original scapular was long length of cloth that went over the front and back shoulders and went to the knees. Originally worn as 'aprons' by the monks scapulars because 'habits' for the various orders and fraternities. Today's devotional scapular is two small squares of cloth, blessed, that hang in front and back that come with specific promises for the faithful that wear them. All of them may bear religious images or text. This might be a difficult one if you haven't been exposed to the Catholic faith.

## Which of the following is not recommended method of disposing of UNHOLY items, such as an Ouija board.

The more the board is used, and made "active" by such use, the more profane the board is. The consequences for improperly disposing of the board, of course, will be more severe when the board has been effectively more used for a longer period of time.

### a)     Bury in a remote location

This can be done sure, and it is the safest and easiest way. Don't touch it; treat it like a dead animal carcass. I say it is they safest because these others provide a certain risk to you or another. We might put in into a bag, but we don't want to preserve it so well in protective plastic bag for example, when it is buried.
We do want over time for the board to decay to turn to mulch. Although this might be the 'safest' method, it still is better recommended to have the board handled in

the way I describe, with the proper prayers and actions to bind the spirit.

### b)  Conceal it in a bag, and put it out in the trash.

Because of whom might uncover this, this is to be avoided. Never assume somewhere your garbage and discarded item will not be uncovered after it leaves you house. "Identity Theft" for example, this is why we shred documents.

### c)  Burn it.

Risky unless the rite steps are taken and this is better reformed by one who is more "pious" like any blessing or deliverance. Say you protection prayers, bind the spirit. Bless the board, and say breaking curse prayers to break any resulting affects and attachments. (*The Prayers are in my "Handbook"*)

### d)  Have it blessed, then store it away in a safe place

This can be done, but "blessing it" is the same as with Burning it. You want to be sure this is done right by the right person. But this isn't the safest, because it can still affect other. We have to pay attention to any and all possible scenarios, these variables might apply to Murphy's law: If anything can go wrong, it will. Our job is to eliminate these possibilities as so this can't be true.

### e) All of the above

As all are not the 'safest' some are not recommended, in the least at all.

### f) None of the above

Comments:
It is better to have Clergy do blessings and other rituals which might stir up in the least these spirits. Catholic Clergy for example have a more pious lifestyle and are spiritually ready for this type of work. You can always say breaking curses prayers to break any attachments, and prayers of protection before taking action to dispose of the Ouija board. Handle it like a 'cursed item'.

## What is the best description of "Purgatory" that is most universally understood by those of ALL faiths?

### a) A temporary hell

For some it maybe, imagine if Mass Murderer *John Wayne Gasey* escape hell by some grace of God. We could easily assume that his penance and 'unfinished business' so-to-speak wouldn't be a mild one. He would have many lessons to learn that he failed to in life.

**b)    A Roman Catholic Myth designed to "sell" indulgences (or a one way pass to 'Go to Heaven').**

Even now as some revert to a modern translation of the Decree on Purgatory by the Council of Trent, 25th session, 1563, The Council simply affirms the existence of purgatory as Christ taught it to the apostles. This originally based on the Jewish tradition of praying for the deceased. The Council sternly instructs that preachers not push beyond that and infer anything that will distract, confuse, and mislead the faithful with unnecessary speculations concerning the nature and duration of purgatorial punishments. Today's Catholic doesn't support this error in Gregory's part to try to place a value on the monies clearly to draw in more donations and support his 'indulgences'.

**c)    A phase of existence between this world and heaven**

This is really the best definition of what is 'universally understood', it's short and sweet. That is why I use this more in order not to have to go into historical references or get shut down by people who don't want understand the concept at all. Know that a "Label" such a purgatory, some consider a red flag and ignore everything that is factual that is detailed beyond this 'written' word.

### d) A place of penance and restitution

As the question says to all faiths we search for something more universally understood. According to the doctrine of the Catholic teaching, this is the state or place of *purification* of *temporary punishment* by which those who die in a state of grace are believed to be made ready for the Beatific Vision in Heaven. To tell them there is an alternate existence beyond a mere heaven and hell is a good first step. This is partially true.

### e) A place of fire and brimstone to atone through suffering.

Though Scripture tells us we will pass through the 'fire of purification', this isn't about atonement. The problem with many preachers have, is they preach to all as though we will all respond the same way. McGregor's theory X would have an employer using 'negative' motivation for employees of a company. "Not getting fired" or fear of a 'suspension' or other 'disciplinary action' might better motivate some to work harder' or to 'not call in sick so often'. But for others it begins to draw disrespect and resentment, thus it is counter productive. Therefore we are all not the same, same as telling don't do that [commit this or that sin] or you will go to hell. Might at some point push one away from our loving God. It is too often propping up the notion of an angry God, not a loving God. Unfortunately, most Priests don't preach or detail purgatory, in part so people don't begin to relax and do just enough to keep themselves "out of hell" thinking purgatory is a fallback or safety net. This is not encouraged, and it is a dangerous notion, as one might still fall short of heaven and even purgatory. It is our daily choice to try to follow the commandments and live as good Christian life to aim our sights on heaven. We are to act as though there is no fail safe plan for us if we miss it.


**Ghosts are not mentioned in the bible . (T/F)**

-False! Nowhere are 'ghosts' specifically mentioned. In the King James Bible translation 'Holy Ghost' is mentioned 89 times.

**Comment:**
Beyond the common "Witch of Endor" passage we also find Ghosts referenced:  **Luke 24:38-40** Look at my hands and my feet. It is I myself! Touch me and see; a ghost does not have flesh and bones, as you see I have."
**Luke 24:36-38** They were startled and frightened, thinking they saw a ghost. **Mark 6:48-50** but when they saw him walking on the lake, they thought he was a ghost. They cried out, **Matthew 14:25-27** When the disciples saw him walking on the lake, they were terrified. "It's a ghost," they said, and cried out in fear.

**1 John 4 1** Dear friends, <u>do not believe every spirit, but test the spirits to see whether they are from God,</u> because many false prophets have gone out into the world. This is how you can recognize the Spirit of God: Every spirit that acknowledges that Jesus Christ has come in the flesh is from God. This might apply because a human spirit might come to you as a "false prophet. The "Test" is using Jesus name, as I talk about in detail, even 'testing' supposed UFO alien visitors, and see how they run when Jesus name is spoken to reveal they are not Aliens from outer space in those cases.

**By its correct definition, what is a ghost?**

**a)  Any "spirit".**

Some might use this word for any visible spirit visitation. However, in doing so is confusing to others, as it is not common to use the word in this way.

**b)  A ghost is a demon, always a demon.**

Those whom believe this need to not work in spiritual warfare, knowing good from bad is basic discernment, a gift from the Holy Spirit, not common to most whom claim to be doing this line of work.

**c)  An echo from the past, (always something residual, nothing "intelligent)**

You'll find no pseudo-Science answer here. This really comes from a certain lack of an understanding as to these 'purgatory' scenarios a spirit might be personally experiencing in the after life. It is rather silly to assume it is some animated, detailed residual energy that doesn't seem to dissipate simply because it doesn't seem to interact or have intelligence. Again we say that there is intelligence behind every one of these types of hauntings, and these apparitions are being witnessed for a reason. God is allowing it for his own reason, It isn't just some mindless recording in time naturally playing back.

**d)     A human spirit**

This is the most true, a ghost by definition is an apparition of a dead person that is believed to appear or become manifest to the living usually as a very shadowy or nebulous image. Sometimes is can be one you don't recognize by its amorphous features.

**e)     Manifested energy.**

More of a 'new age', atheistic pseudo-science answer


**By definition what are the "Nephilim"?**

**a)     Demonic beings made from human sperm**

What a horrid thought that the incubus impregnates its willing victims using the collected discarded sperm of human males. I couldn't find validation for this, it may be another myth. I can't see a psychical collection and preservation of the sperm and find it is effective. The unholy act of mating with a female I feel is in part a mockery of more satanic or 'fringe' beliefs. This is more a notion that comes from those who study from the wrong side of Demonology reading Gnostics texts, The Satanic bible, Demons of the Flesh etcetera.

### b)  The fallen angels

The Nephilim are <u>physical beings</u>, the fallen angels are angelic/spiritual beings without a body.

### c)  A race of giant humans

This answer is the most 'true'. As in Genesis "There were Giants in those day, referring to the time of Noah", Numbers 13:32 "and all the people whom we saw in it are men of great size. There also we saw the Nephilim (the sons of Anak are part of the Nephilim); and we became like grasshoppers in our own sight; and so we were in their sight." Even though these giants were called the Nephilim there is much confusion as to whether they were of human origin of 'great men of size' or of a 'supernatural spiritual nature'. Early sources refer to the 'sons of heaven' as 'Angels' The earliest such references seem to be in the apocrypha of the Dead Sea Scrolls, the Greek and Aramaic Enochic literature as well as Jubilees.

### d) Demonic-human hybrids

Half-man half-demonic beasts, in the *days of Noah,* this 'life-form' was believed to be infesting the planet. Some believe that the same was true for animals as well.

### e) UFO aliens

If the UFO theory of "Flying saucers" is some how correct, I don't think these "Close encounters" are these same beings. There are enough indications of that when you look closely. And as I said, why do they fear Jesus name like demons?

### f) Inter-dimensional beings.

If you think about it, Angels, demons, ghosts, 'are "Inter-dimensional" beings' already. But, in this when people say 'shadow people' might be this, they are thinking more in terms of "people from other worlds" like our own as in 'Aliens". No, this does not apply to the Nephilim.

## What is the ultimate goal of the demonic?

### a) World domination

If you read your bible, this pretty much sums it up. They all seek to deceive, divide and destroy God's creations. Anything they can do to accomplish that end would better serve them to their true agenda.

**b)    Your physical death**

Only if you physical death would possibly ensure your spiritual death. Or somehow your death serves their greater battle. Such as if they were able to kill a priest. If they someone didn't know who Jesus was the whole time, to them, they would just be killing a "Saint", who is spreading the truth and messages that are undermining their goals. So to them to have Jesus killed in any way possible would serve them.

**c)    To influence humans to further empower evil.**

It is part of their strategy of course to try to affect those in power, even on a lower level such as your supposed friends who lend a hand in their 'temptations'. Humans can serve the demonic in a variety of ways and not even be aware their are being 'used' as a 'pawn' or a mere 'instrument' of the dark side. They will do anything to help lend a hand to your spiritual destruction. We can see how Friends and even family might work for their side on issues such as a 'push' towards choice that lead to "abortion" or a "divorce" that is no way justified.

**d)    Your spiritual death**

In simple terms they interact and affect our world to aim for our "spiritual death". Which is to become a

"Condemned spirit", a lost soul whom has no chance at heaven, their fate is sealed.

### e) To get even with God

Surely to take another soul from God and heaven is a victory for them. To them this lends a certain morbid satisfaction, in part, because they hate God and appear to detest all his creation.

**If you had to choose one, which is the best to carry daily for 'personal' protection?**

### a) Saint Michael Medal

A bit of a tricky question, but the Saint Benedict requires no action; just wear it on a chain around your neck. Because of its 'silent' protection, this one is be the single best choice. And you can even wear it to bed and in the shower (we strongly!).

### b) Blessed Salt

I don't generally say to carry salt for personal 'protection'. It is part of our arsenal for personal protection. But it is a matter of including it in you wallet or pocket without a worry of it going through the 'wash', and the bag can break open.

### c) Holy water

As with the sea salt, this one might be good for an "In case of emergency use", however, again, it is not all that easy to carry a vial of Holy water around. So it isn't really practical for a 24/7 protection.

### d) A Bible

The Bible itself alone isn't going to act for personal protection just having it on oneself. It's not what's in the pages; it's what is in your heart that provided the protection. How about the size restriction? Men don't carry hand bags and a briefcase might be forgotten.

### e) A Rosary

The rosary might provoke more than to protect at first, in part the rosary is significant because:
**1)** It is often blessed
**2)** Your own prayers 'energizes' it as though it is an 'extra' blessing giving it life though the faith and plea of the spoken entreaty.
**3)** The crucifix that is typically attached on the rosary. We don't carry rosaries to protect our selves it might be more something to provoke, not as much as sprinkling holy water, but it can be in your pocket.

# What do we more commonly find with EVP and demonic spirits?

### a) Demonic spirits like to ensure fear with "growls"

The reason they might leave a trace of their presence with a "guttural growl" is not 100 percent clear. Is it merely to intimidate you, or to install a certain fear into the listeners/ field investigators or more importantly to STOP the priest or deliverance minister from completing the prayers of blessing or Exorcism. Such evidence might be allowed so that the listeners will get a clue to try to get help. It might also make some more curious, whom for the "trophy" of it alone, will try to capture more on audio tape to prove something. Provoking instances like this can ultimately make things worse.

### b) Spirits are *shy*, you have to beckon them to respond to grab captures.

Believe it or not, I actually heard this one from a self-described "Psychic-Medium". I just hope I don't need to tell you this is ridiculous.

### c) A sort of spirit 'prime directive' prevents spirits from leaving physical evidence, except under rare circumstances.

This does hold *some* truth, but it works as a sort of "Cosmic Law". For demons and their minions, human invitation opens up their ability to manifest in this world and more affect us and our physical world. Most often the demon you might have encounter is not working here at full power, it has some level of restriction. Demons are subject to God and his will, never forget that! Even when they can move a refrigerator across the floor, usually what they can really do is really limited. A "prime directive", meaning the most prominent guiding principle, is a term some "Star Trek" fans understand as when another Culture *'visits'* the directive is purposely not to affect their culture with your technology and habits. You would *visit* without introducing anything more than your polite customs. I am not sure if this is a good reference but it has been used before, and metaphorically, it is a good comparison. However, that THEY don't make this choice, God restricts them to the extent of what they can do in our physical world.

**d)    Digital recorders don't work as well as Analog**

This isn't a topic relating to technology of "Tape" versus, "Digital". Although some will say Analog is better for results. ;)


**Jack and Jim are debating, Jack says most cases are demonic in nature, Jim says most are not. Who is more correct?**

   a)    **Jim** – See below

   b)    **Jack** – See below

**c)     Neither one**

See below where we go into detail.

**d)     Both are right as there are only opinions in these matters**

Beware of this philosophy of nonsense, it will come up in many discussions you may have online and in person being the general topic of conversation. Each person can only answer according to their experience and their conscious. According to our experience and faith beliefs as well as to the educational purposes of this book, almost all exposure to supernatural spirits *will* be of the Demonic. Never assume otherwise for to do so could jeopardize your client as well as yourself in any investigation. Don't say this out loud, don't tell the client this right away, investigate, rule everything else out and contact clergy when you are positive it could be nothing else.

**If Jack is somehow right which of these statements apply:**

**a)     A demonic is 'calling the shots' behind most haunted cases, although it hasn't itself manifested at the haunted location as an "infestation" or later stage.**

The question by passes this since this isn't 'demonic' in nature, since no demonic spirit has yet manifested. Even though the case may be that the human spirit might be working for the demonic. The "Boss" or "puppet-master" isn't here. It is working from their realm.

**b) Any "haunting" would have to be demonic since it is clear in the bible that all will either pass into "hell" or "heaven" upon death.**

This thought process disallows the possibility of what we call a 'purgatory' spirit appearing in a limited capacity for a very limited time. We can't know the mind of God and what he will allow nor test the Spirit when we haven't even established that there actually even *is* a spirit there. Don't ever put the cart before the horse and make assumptions on facts not in evidence.

**c) Jack in referring to the majority of cases that contact him for help, where he specializes in 'demonic' or more severe haunting cases.**

Generalizing based on your specific areas of haunted cases, is not in itself an accurate statistic. Some make this mistake in asking *"Why do the Warrens find a demonic haunting everywhere they go?"* The ones that made it into their books and the lectures are notably demonic. What about the other few thousand times it was *NOT* demonic? They don't mention them as much and people don't care to hear about these because they are in fact less "horrific". This is true.

**d) Jack is heavily rooted in the fundamental beliefs, and is not speaking from case study or experience.**

Very true, some will experience something once and label all encounters as so conform to this absolute belief. We've heard of one case where a person discovered a (demonic) 'spirit was talking to them on the Ouija board, it wasn't spelling correctly, they decided to go around saying "demons can't spell on the board" as if it were the gospel truth. It probably is *to them*, it is patently absurd and goes against everything we know of demons.

**If Jim, is somehow right, what would apply to his statement?**

**a) Most cases do not have a demonic sprit that have actually 'manifested'.**

I agree with this, there are enough indications that this is true. However, we should note we might take the same solution in using Deliverance to rid the home of this spirit(s). But the battle won't be so hard fought. Also we note it doesn't get affected so much by religious symbols as a demon does. We rely more on rebuking with prayers and blessings to remove them. This is directly asking Jesus, the Angels and Saints to 'bind' our unwanted visitor out of the home and off the property. Bind it so it may not return, and bless the place so it cannot re-enter and dwell there again.

**b)   Demons do not exist outside of hell's domain, therefore they can't affect this world.**

This line of thinking will not help you in this healing ministry. This is false. If Christ ordered us to expel demons who are we to argue they don't exist?

**c)   Jim has never run into a true demonic case.**

If this is true but there are not enough indications to say this is true based on his statement alone. Jim's observations from experience, might have lead him to incorrectly believe in his statement.

**d)   Jim simply does not believe in the existence of evil spirits or demons.**

We have both heard many people say this, and while they are harboring such beliefs about the existence of demons they still believe in prayer and heaven. Which alone should serve alone be a strong indication to not listen to Jim and what he says, since it is filled with based on a "bias", not a true "knowledge" or "understanding".

e) **Jim lacks a level of personal experiences or has not correctly learned from them.**

Since I lean to "Jim's statement as the one that is "mostly true", we have to realize, that regardless of where he gets this information, it doesn't change the fact that the statement is more true.

f) **Jim is a pseudo-science type who clings blindly to residual haunt theories, and notions there is not life after death.**

His opinion doesn't matter in your investigation, or study, just as with #d, this bias will only confuse and interfere with your understanding of the real truth. You have to know when to listen and depend to science/medicine/rational and when to simply ignore it.

**In the Book, where I make mention of "cause and effect" I am referring to?**

a) **Testing the spirits with provocation as to get an EVP**

Certainly testing for a condition is a "cause and affect" scenario, however, this is not to what I am referring to in the book.

**b) How demonic spirits will by default react to certain words, and objects.**

This is true since they can be expected to always advert to the presence of holy symbols and certain words.

**c) How our actions will directly invite and empower a demonic spirit into our lives.**

This is related to an action and its direct consequences.

**d) Of how cleansings/blessings of a 'haunted location' is affecting the level of activity.**

It is not related to a specific act as I refer to in the book, this is not the correct answer.

**e) How there is a lack of "cause and effect" under a scientific conditions when observing supposed haunted people or locations.**

To recap, in the book I refer to how we can determine the very nature of demons how they seem to respond to religious provocation. Such as the way the name of Jesus, or the sprinkling of holy water, will send them running or force them to reveal themselves and their true nature.

**Which of the following does not apply to my statement of: "Our words are binding"?**

**a) Cursing at someone.**

We might bless our children, the words have literal meanings. Remember when either using curse words or issuing a curse directed at someone can have negative affects at well. If you purposely or accidentally curse someone it's best to see reconciliation and discuss this with your clergy before attempting this work.

**b) Telling someone on your deathbed that you will watch over them for as long as they live.**

Our words are indeed binding, more than on one occasion a lingering spirit might be there because a promises of this kind. The notion "unfinished business" is often a correct assumption in those trying to understand one reason why a ghost might linger here. So this observation is true in this case.

**c) Prayers**

Prayers, the opposite of curses, designed to call upon God or asking for intercession from his angels and Saints. The more we pray the more it affects us, those around us and the people we pray for positively.

### d) Promises made in the form of "Vows"

A vow is a covenant usually between two. I mention how ordination/pastoral vows are more of a covenant with God. Taking sincere vows to serve our Lord in this way is a great blessing and a great sacrifice at the same time.

### e) Lies, slander, "false witnesses".

This does not apply.

## What other "demonic stages" did I add to the list of the initial three that were introduced by some books such as Gerald Brittle's book *"The Demonologist"*?

## Temptation

The sublime manipulation that we are subjected to through out our entire lives, no one is immune including those priests, clergy, nuns, monks or any other order or fraternity under the clerical service to God. It will steadily increase as we become more "demonized" approaching later stages, it can be so strong the imagery of the temptations can begin to come to us as hallucinations, as though you are dreaming while you are awake.

## Scout and Roam
See below

## And Demonic Death/Murder

When it moved from possession to murder or suicide, this is one step past possession. The "End game" which might be merely a desperate move to not leave this earthly plane empty handed.

**Which of the following will NOT open you up for a "Demonic retaliation", when assisting a client:**

### a) Talking to them on the phone

This has happened far too often, even with certain "radio show" guests I have had on, but that was over a speaker phone as well. Be careful

### b) e-mail contact only.

Something as minute as this could affect you directly, some cases are severe, not even responding to the e-mail, just reading it can bring something with it. This is *very rare*. But note an action by you versus simply reading a message or internet post, without action to reply or to help, will usually not draw anything of a "retaliation" to you or your family. But this is their point, to try to discourage you from helping them, and of course when you do "nothing" there is no reason for them to try to punish you for intervening?

**c)    Solely offering prayers for them.**

Anytime we take any sort of action we might incur an opposing "action". The more severe the case(s) will draw more severe of a "payback".

**d)    Sending 'Sacramentals' and prayers by postal mail.**

Correspondence does seem to be more "infectious", how ever in any level you are "meddling" with the affairs of the demons. These demons won't take that lightly. We assume any form of contact; even "one way" will possibly affect us. So we try to 'break" and "Bind" these spirit attachments, and say protection prayers before an initial contact.

**e)    All of the above**

In how all of these things can affect the client in the least bit, they all may draw some form of "Payback" from an offending demonic spirit.

**f)    None of the above**
Also refer to my comments on #e.

Comments:

*Some will notice more "retaliation" simply because they are not meant to intervene; God has not "called" them to do this extreme work. This is what I call it when it "Rubs you the wrong way" these people will pay dearly for the little they might do in helping clients. They are more venerable because as one entirely self appointed to do this work, they will be the hardest hit, not having a special grace from God that better assists them in the work and protects them better from such evil. This is why we deeply consider **Not** doing the work, rather than to jump out there after a Ghost hunting course or successfully completing this demonology test. You can pay with your life, not just your finances. Always daily say your spiritual warfare prayer(s), the battle is not over simply because the client is free, they never forget your meddling!*


## How many spirits can "possess a human at one time?

### a) Only one at a time

I heard this from one professing that when the Holy Spirit dwells within, there is no room for more than one spirit, such as a 'demon'. First of all the holy spirit dwells within all humans to some degree, regardless if you are Christian or not. God created us in his image so he created his spirit into us. Second, this notion is based on what? Some notion there "Isn't room" for another spirit (excluding your own spirit/soul). Again, we don't think in terms of a 3D world, a "lack of space" won't be a reason for spirit to not enter. And the Holy Spirit won't vacate the body until after death. In the book it was discussed that there have been records of people being possessed by 'legion' meaning "3,000 -6,000" and that number could very well go higher.

**b)    If they are "Christian"** *only* **the Holy Spirit will dwell within.**

This may be true, but when it comes down to it is all ultimately Gods will. And living fully a Christian life, is a good template of prevention.

**c)    up to "six"**

Although the number six might lean toward being a demonic number, it is not a designation as to the limited number of spirits that might be present at one time in the possessed.

**d)    A "Legion"**

Legion is used in the bible to represent a Roman Legion of soldiers which could number from 3000 to 6000 men. We find that these entities might speak as a "collective" and not as individuals; therefore they are speaking of the legion they are part of. Just as sometimes they will cite their general in a higher demon, that are typically referred to as "Devils". When the exorcist ask the demon to identify itself it may be answer with the name of this higher rank devil, rather than its own supposed individual name.

### e) The number is unknown

Can we assess a limitation? It is currently unknown as to how many might inhabit an individual at one time. We first have to understand our 3 dimension 'limited mentality' does not apply in the spirit realm. Less severe cases more often will have 1-6 demons, the Brookfield Demon case was said to have 'forty-two' in one individual.

## What is a "Scout and roam"?

### a) A ghost might travel with you, wherever you go

Although this can occur, it is not what I am referring to by "Scout and roam", which is referring to Demons and their minions.

### b) A demon that has no limitations or boundaries in its travels.

The limitations and boundaries are set by God. When we choose 'sinful' activities or turn away from leading an 'honest and charitable' life *we* open these boundaries up by our actions. Demons are not free to go anywhere they choose. They can not simply be in close proximity of places more 'positive' with good and Gods grace.

### c) When a demonic spirit has presented itself, but is not in the least infesting the home.

This is true, this wandering stage where they might even appear on a night you have worked on a case and followed you in the door. Sometimes the visit is a warning, an attempt to frighten you. A "Payback" or some form of retaliation as we would see it. But it may not be an infestation. Before infestation, stages of this sort of scouting might be in a way to test the waters. You are allowed by God to witness some occurrences or see the shadowy visitors so you can take immediate action. Most often they would certainly choose to sneak in totally undetected, but it is within God laws that require some signs of their presence and their "coming'.

### d) A demonic spirit that has not been given "invitation" to show itself.

In a way we might invite it just from dealing with a case, even if it is a visit for certain "retaliation", intervening on behalf of the client had provoke the spirit to in the least be curious about you perhaps. So in a way you invited/allowed it in, just not officially as it is referred to at the threshold of a demonic infestation.

### e)    A spirit that affects more than one person, and at more than one location.

This is different that what the Scout and roam" stage is defined to be.

<u>Comment:</u>
"Scout and Roam" is the second stage of demonic influence that I outline in my first book. For example, if you are working on a demonic case, and get a visitor before you even visit the client. This is an example of a "scout and roam" stage. If nothing is done, it could very well move to an infestation over time for some. Many do not know that the early warning signs of an infestation, are actually this scout and roam, where the demons test the waters, leave 'not so obvious' calling cards, symbolic of the coming infestation. If you do not rebuke them, do not pray, have your house blessed regularly this is an invitation for more demonic occurrences.


## A "Religious Demonologist"…

### a)…Is a title created by the Catholic Church…

To our knowledge this title is not used within the ranks of the Roman Catholic church officially publicly or otherwise by Laity, or clergy at this time. It is a often misused title self given by many 'ghost hunters' who have heard something go 'bump' they thought was a demon and now consider themselves an 'authority' on the subject.

**b)…Was a title abolished in 1577 along with the office of the inquisitor.**

This was the last known indication such a title *"Demonologist"* was being officially used by the church. If you ask some Bishops or Priests about this title, this is what they will tell you. There is limited training out there even for the very educated Clergy in the Catholic Church. There are very few that decide to specialize in "Demons 101" while in Rome for training.

**c)…Is a title created by Author Gerald Brittle to describe the unique work Ed Warren would do as "Laity".**

The actual title prefix with the word "Religious" demonologist" affix onto it was in fact created by author Gerald Brittle for his book **"The Demonologist"**, which was to describe the unusual work Ed Warren did as laity. Ed Warren also hung a shingle outside his house that said: "Demonologist Witchcraft Specialist". Often work was directed to him by the local archdiocese when they were unable to ascertain there was a need for a priest or exorcist….

**d)…Is a valid title for anyone who studies "demonology"**

By definition the word "Demonologist" ( the study of demons) would mean yes, but in this we are referring to 'Religious Demonologist" as the word religious in the title which changes its meaning. Note that in the mainstream world of 'ghost hunters' and pop culture junkies, many do not consider a "demonologist" to be merely a student study of these topics, but a "specialist" when hearing this term they would believe that this 'specialist' is either on the side of Judeo-Christianity or from the older usage where it is referring to one who conjures demons to do their biddings.

**e) All of the above** – does not apply


**A child is afraid to sleep at night, he says there are black "monsters" that come out of his closet at night. Which one stands alone as the better advice?**

**a)     Tell them to ignore them, and try to go back to sleep.**

This seems a bit to detailed in its description to simply tell a child it is best to "ignore" it. Although this may be what you do as to not frighten the child. Give them a Saint Benedict medal and a Miraculous medal for example on a separate and unrelated occasion. Pray with the child and teach them the power of how 'good' they feel after prayer. That is until you can take care of this supposed monster yourself, all done discreetly. I recommend do a blessing while they are out or at school, and no matter if it is just a dream or real. You can also silently pray it behind the scenes "just-in-case" and you consider these steps as well while they are away:

**1)** Clean up under his/her bed and his closet, his room. The Devil loves chaos and disorder; he counts on it for confusion.

2) Say the 'hedge prayer of protection' for example to get/keep you protected.

3) Better you yourself to have and wear a Saint Benedict medal on yourself the whole while as well.

4) Open a window and pray a blessing in the room.
With holy water sprinkle in his closet and all over the room "In the name of Jesus and by his precious blood, begone! And leave this place go back to the world you came from and never return! Say three times, sprinkle a second time under the bed a third over the room door way. You may have to do this more than once so be prepared to repeat as necessary. This is a more mild way to deal with this, better to 'flush' it out of your house, doing it in all rooms.

5) If you want to smudge the place use genuine Frankincense and myrrh blessed by a priest (aka 'high mass' incense) and go through each and every room with it smoldering, systematically painting the potential spirits into a corner. Interestingly, even if

you have no lurking shadows, it will mellow out the stress and cover a feeling of well being in the house for a while. So you have nothing to lose taking these precautions.

6) Prevention: hang a blessed St Benedict crucifix in their room. Anoint the door way with holy water, in the name of the father, son and Holy Spirit. Place a Saint Benedict medal under his mattress as well.

## b) Tell the child those monsters are real, and tell him how to deal with them.

At this stage you are only dealing with fleeting shadows that haven't touched the child. You don't need to be so up front with this reality do consider a child's fragile psyche. When we say "Monsters" it is referring to demonic/evil spirits. Avoid telling them, and go as long as possible, because their fear will make matters worse, and be more traumatizing

## c) Do nothing, and tell him to not be afraid and to be a "man" about it.

Ok, what parent would give their child a snake when he asked for lunch? You can try to have a child deal with school bullies this way, even then and it is bad advice. Imagine if a serial killer is luring kids into his car in your neighborhood, and the police haven't yet caught him yet. How would "being a man about it" help? He is too young to defend or protect himself on many levels and does not possess the tools either spiritually and physically.

**d) Tell him there are no such thing as Ghost and monsters. Again do nothing.**

This is not a good choice entirely, to say this is the same as telling him, you are "Imagining things"; "you are crazy"; "You are dreaming". In essence you are telling the child that you don't believe them. A terrified child knows what they are seeing and if you are not there for them in the right way this could all get so much worse quicker than you can imagine!

**e)   Tell him he is a Christian and there is nothing to fear.**

A Baptism helps removes demons from the past and protects on many levels. We are in a new arena where some adult was exposed to something and now a new thing is testing the waters by coming to visit the child. Don't ever assume that a mere christening is good for an entire lifetime of spiritual warfare. This is a foolhardy. Just as some Christians feel they will go to heaven automatically 'no matter what', because "Jesus died for our sins", because "it say's so in the bible" and "I'm a baptized good Christian".   Remember Hitler? He murdered thousands of Priests, Jewish, gypsies etc. being a professed or devout Christian. That designation with not by default make you bullet proof!

## f) Teach him prayers, etc. without saying what they are for.

If you remember "Cujo" that Steven king movie, the boy was afraid of a "monster in his closet" as it is told in the beginning of the book and the movie. The parents came up with special "the monster words". The problem here is these words were more like something for a fantasy of nursery rhyme and not an actual prayer. Kind of like Dumbo's feather except the outcome is much more deadly than a Disney film. Teach them a prayer of protection, have them memorize it and place it by their bed. Here are two prayers they can say, you always leave in the names of "Jesus" but we can doctor up words like "evil spirits" so they don't expect ghosts. Satan and his minions can be explained to be something working not as ghosts or spirits for the time being.

Comments:
We should always be are of our children's 'spiritual state' and life in general including stressors, divorce, or problems at school. Do they seem like something is bothering them lately? These things might draw in these spirits more or be a part of their after affects. Who is your child playing with and what are they watching on the media (TV or Movies) MONITOR their lives! What goes into that innocent head will come out again somehow and someway. Be the best parent you can be over all in paying attention to your child is the best medicine of prevention. We both have had situations come up with our children and have had to take stricter

stances on things such as TV – We got rid of it 3 years ago for this very reason. Children's programs have some of the 'raciest' and suggest ads attached. These ads are aimed at 'entertaining' most of us adults who are 'desensitized' to the content and suggestions that are not the morals you may want to raise your family with! Be watchful – this is what Christ compels us to do!

**If you want to discuss your child's situation, contact us at:   help@catholicdemonologist.com**


**Why do some warn that you shouldn't deal with "demonic" haunting cases unless you have a calling?**

**a)   As to be obedient to the 'Christian Church'**

An obedience to the 'Christian church would be to *not* do it at all as they prefer NO LAITY does this work at all – ever, end of conversation. It is too dangerous for them to allow you to make such a call with anyone, unless they *are sure* they *do* have the proper training. Just look at how the church appoints and anoints exorcists, "Bishops", Cardinals and the Pope.  No laity interested in pursuing this line of work should automatically expect to be recognized by the church, just because they might have contacted a local Bishop or other clergy to help start the "red tape" towards a church sanctioned exorcism. Unless you have followed the 'appropriate chain of authority'  (as Christ calls us to)  and they decide take your word for it, and don't have to conduct a long and lengthy investigation Don't expect to be welcomed with open arms by any church clergy. But getting things started should be enough here unless you are another of the 'media hounds' are looking to appear at conventions, start a 'demonic museum' like the Warrens and play as though you are an appointed "religious demonologist". If this is the case, this healing ministry is not for you.

**b)   You don't pick the work, it picks you.**

This is true to a big extent. God does not call the qualified – he qualifies those he calls. Then again we may also have had no indications at all in our life history into our adult years that we have some sort of healing "calling".

**c)   If you don't have a true "calling" from God to do this work, you will be 'affected' by these spirits in the worse way.**

Oh yes, this is true whether you decide to follow this line of ministry or not. The temptations of the devil will be there for our entire years on this earth. This 'calling' will call more attention to you on a spiritual plane than you can imagine. God and his Angels and Saints will help to guide you to diagnosing and helping solve these situations if you are truly operating within God's calling. And with the extra prayers and seeking God daily, with that comes extra protection, you might see it as an extra guardian angel(s). The truths is when you take vows and make a covenant with God for a life commitment, this is more than just the typical Baptismal, Confirmed Catholic that attends church once a week for example. It would be good to try to surrender your life to God on a higher level, not necessarily as a clergyman. In a way some of these other orders that help laity who will not receive Holy Orders to achieve desired levels of spirituality. I would recommend you join one groups of these and not an internet org or some other fly-by-night 'drive through' event, you want something you can attend 'in person' and go to regularly. We're talking about the importance of a spiritual mentor, advisor and earthly confidant you can trust all your scariest moments with, who will be there to comfort you and guide you with the tough decisions.


**The Blessed Virgin Mary, is significant in "deliverance" and exorcisms because: (choose the answer that is the most true)**

**a)　She is the Mother of Jesus.**

True, and it does make her special over all others whom have lived on earth and are still to come. "Blessed are you among Woman" , note: "All generations shall call me blessed"

**b)　More so because the history of the Catholic Church and their honor and veneration of Mary.**

Not relevant, as this is saying it is only a matter of church opinion or doctrine, and not something that has a strong affect against evil. Mary is not worshiped, but honored as a Holy intercessor.

**c) Her Purity is a mantle of grace and light against these powers of darkness.**

True, and is one reason, as I describe in the book, "Positive" against "Negative" "Purity" repeals these unclean spirits of darkness. The only surviving victim of the 'obsessed' or possessed "Ted Bundy" cases survived (she claims) be the direct intervention of the Blessed Virgin Mary and praying the rosary to her. We all need light in dark places and what better to have than an all loving accepting mother who never leaves our side in our darkest hours.

**d) Her hierarchy in heaven.**

Although this is a supposed issue of "rank", and she does take precedence over even Saint Michael in heaven, we are looking for the reason *why* she is a powerful intercessor for spiritual warfare in this question more so.

**e) Because she is a female saint.**
This question is not relevant to gender.

**f) As Satan used a woman to bring the fall of man, God used a woman to help bring the fall of Satan.**

Beyond Mary's purity and perfection, and hierarchy, it is clear that God has intended Mary to be used in defense of her son's Church and his people against the powers of evil. "Woman behold thy son, [To John] behold they Mother" She has been given to the world as our spiritual mother. Her peace, patience, love and suffering have not gone unnoticed in other religions. She is venerated as a mother for all.

# III – BOOK SUPPLIMENTAL MATERIAL.

## 1. THE AFFECTS OF THE "BLESSED SACRAMENT".

As Catholics we should never forget about the Blessed Sacrament, which is certainly the "Holiest of Holies" since Jesus ascended into heaven ( this is one of the great 'mysteries' of the church). The power of the presence can be a silent therapy, a great way to prep before the battle. A great peace can come from sitting in this true presence, those suffer from the loss of love ones, going through hard ships, divorce even will find and unusual inner peace, that otherwise seems to not surface. Even from talking with friends, or distracting oneself with movies and activities. Our one-ness getting closer to Jesus will help with the battles that lie ahead, and are ongoing throughout life.

Here are some tips to truly get the affect of the positive presence of Jesus while visiting the Blessed Sacrament

  **a)**  Find out when you local church has these "adoration" hours scheduled. It is usually in your church bulletin.

  **b)**  You should spend at least <u>one hour</u> in front.

c) Open your mind and picture Jesus the image of Jesus over-laid onto the bread there-in.

d) Don't read or preoccupy yourself, focus on Jesus only.

e) The more you are in turmoil the more you should attend. I knew a fellow going through divorce whom found that attending daily for 2 hours gave him the peace he needed to get through a tough time in his life.

As you recall how I refer to the "Proximity affect" being close to such a "positive" energy as the blessed sacrament, can have a cleansing affect. In a month of daily adoration, done properly, one can emerge a changed man. Old emotional/psychological scars healed. I should also note that anytime you show up, you are helping to support these special hours of devotion. Be sure to sign the log if you show up, even if it is for only 1 minute. The way the budgets are in parishes now, they don't seem to place such an importance on energy bills lighting, and heating or cooling a small chapel or space in the church. So this can help ensure the Blessed Sacrament will be available for others as well.

## OF A DISCERMENT OF GOOD SPIRITS
(WHEN GOOD SEEMS EVIL)

If an said location is indeed truly haunted, consider that a at least one human is affected somehow, someway. It is only by God's express will that anyone is aware of any supposed haunting and we should consider that.

More importantly is to properly discern good from evil, and not rely on your senses, something apparently good can be a wolf in sheep's clothing. And at times the opposite is true. Saint Faustina (of Poland), in her diary, had told of being visited by a purgatory spirit, flames around the face, an angry look on the face. She recognized the person as a nun whom had died some time recently. She didn't assume this spirit was a minion of the devil, and stepped up prayers for her. The next time the face looked furious, almost frightening and more engulfed in flames. She went further with prayers and offerings still, so as when the third visitation occurred, suddenly it was the nuns face surrounded by light, smiling, and serine. What does this tell us?

We should not assume a spirit is in hell simply because it reveals itself as "angry" and surrounded by "fire".

I can go further and tell how St. Theresa (the Little flower), was known also for her gift of discernment. However, she was to learn hard lessons in how we often can't see through the guise of evil masquerading as "good", that it is a lesson in humility to understand that even with such a gift of the Holy Spirit, you can still be in error. So we all face certain confusion, and we try to use logic, knowledge and reasoning to discern to some level.

As the guidelines in my book hint some indications of "Good" or "evil", of "God" or of the "Devil", still we are extremely limited. We truly rely upon God's grace for true discernment, one may have a history of an apparently correct discernment good from evil, and on one occasion, this supposed "experience" still doesn't justify an "expertise". Yet we find these whom call themselves "Sensitive" or "Psychic-mediums" (ones we usually get exposed to through the media), these individuals are growing in epidemic proportions. I had said in the book in the section speaking of the masquerade, how these spirits like to appear to be children, Also how they can fool all "sixth senses". But the special ability of discernment is not something there to call upon anytime you say "jump", we need to understand that this is because it comes from the Holy Spirit it isn't a "performance on cue" act. And consider how even from the best of us whom have lived the life of a saint, they understood that they have it right all the time. A lesson in humility can be a lesson hard learned and when we are dealing with other people, it can affect then. Bottom line is to pray for discernment, don't assume anything, and place in God's hands.

# PERSISTENCE AND AFTER AFFECTS

In deliverance and spiritual warfare in general, inconsistency is a problem when the client(s) are presented with valid tried and true solutions yet they don't follow through. They may do prescribed prayers for example, after a few days they stop entirely. This even can be from a certain indication of a "peace" and Calm" that now seems to exist, where it was utter chaos just days before. They may be exhausted, and it is not an easy thing to continue onward with words and actions designed to keep the evil from returning and gaining ground, when they just want to put the whole nightmare behind them. We say to have a person assigned as one to oversea their progress into the future, but then we find they may begin to "humor" the inquiries of daily prayers, and weekly mass. So sadly we might hear from them again before 6 months have passed, with a resurgence that might be worse the second time around. It needs to be stressed the importance the practices that prevent the evil from returning again.

A final note on this is if it returns, you might see it has surfaced in another way. Instead of the typical "haunted house" occurrences, some 12-24 months lately another form of the demonic affect can take hold. The husband and wife may be separated, the eldest son is involved with drug abuse, the youngest is shoplifting, The family is in disarray, and to the typical family therapist is just some dysfunctional family. But in the year it had changed them from a very close and loving family. These were not the people you knew a year ago. They relaxed the religion and let it in the way it more often affects all of us, through free will and everyday choice.

Temptation may come at higher levels, harder to resist, but they wear you down well. So even if there is no signs of a typical infestation, we must never forget how they can work in levels of temptation on a much higher level, especially after a family or individual has been once affected at the higher levels. They will always be more venerable to the lesser levels of even mere temptation. And they will have to pray more than they have in their life, prior to the infection and for the rest of their lives. It is like a new diet for one with heart disease. We should not consider this bad, but a way we become closer to God.

# A NOTE ABOUT "POSSESSION CASES"

You might seriously consider entirely dropping a client if they exhibit one or more of these warning signs. It is a waste of your valued time, and you will find that even though they may be truly afflicted it is more they love the attention. At some point you have to know when to back away, and realize that the lord

**a)** Sending you update e-mails, not specifically addressing you individually, you are one of a bulk of correspondences of other people.

**b)** And... The other people being contacted are well known in the media, such as from TV shows like "Paranormal State" (Ryan Buell and PRS), "Ghost hunters", (Jason Hawes and Grant Wilson T.A.P.S., etc.)

**c)** Their local parish priest and others, whom were contacted for counseling and help, have not seen nor heard of him/her yet.

**d)** There is evidence they continue with occult practices they were warned to cease.

**e)** Lies, untruth. They might lie in answering questions relating to the advice you have given. Just to "Humor you" but it is deceiving you into believing they are saying the prayers, going to mass and counseling, etc.

**f)** There continues to be a lack of witnesses to continued stories of experience, entailing paranormal encounters. You can make your own call, but remember *"The Lord helps those who help themselves"*, if they are not cooperating and following sound advice on these matters of the spirit. They have tied your hands. Ed Warren used to say: "You can lead a horse to water, but you can't make him drink", we can add to that and say sometimes one step at a time is what we do, but at times we don't even see they have taken steps forward.

Additional copies of this book can be attained directly by visiting: www.SwordsOfSaintMichael.org

A special bulk price and shipping rate will be quoted based on the number of books ordered.

"The Catholic Demonologist Workbook and Study Guide"

© Copyright 2008-2013 Kenneth Deel,
All rights reserved.

Made in the USA
Middletown, DE
16 September 2015